KB043857

Reading Schedule

이 책은 총 32,000여개의 단어로 구성되어 있습니다.(중복 포함, 1페이지는 대략 171단어)
분당 150단어 읽기는 원어민이 말하는 속도입니다. 먼저 이 기준을 목표로 시작해보세요.

● 1회 읽기

날 짜	/	/	/	/	/
시 간	~	~	~	~	~
페이지	~	~	~	~	~

내용 이해도 ☑ 90%이상 ☑ 70% ☑ 50% ☑ 30%이하

리딩속도 계산	**214**	÷		×	**154**	=	
	전체 페이지		시간(분)		1페이지 당 평균 단어수		분당 읽은 단어수

● 2회 읽기

날 짜	/	/	/	/	/
시 간	~	~	~	~	~
페이지	~	~	~	~	~

내용 이해도 ☑ 90%이상 ☑ 70% ☑ 50% ☑ 30%이하

리딩속도 계산	**214**	÷		×	**154**	=	
	전체 페이지		시간(분)		1페이지 당 평균 단어수		분당 읽은 단어수

● 3회 읽기

날 짜	/	/	/	/	/
시 간	~	~	~	~	~
페이지	~	~	~	~	~

내용 이해도 ☑ 90%이상 ☑ 70% ☑ 50% ☑ 30%이하

리딩속도 계산	**214**	÷		×	**154**	=	
	전체 페이지		시간(분)		1페이지 당 평균 단어수		분당 읽은 단어수

행복한 왕자 外

리딩 속도가 빨라지는 영어책 016

행복한 왕자 外
THE HAPPY PRINCE AND OTHER TALES

2023년 4월 10일 초판 1쇄 인쇄
2023년 4월 15일 초판 1쇄 발행

지은이 오스카 와일드
발행인 손건
편집기획 김상배, 장수경
마케팅 최관호, 김재명
디자인 이재성
제작 최승용
인쇄 선경프린테크

발행처 LanCom 랜컴
주소 서울시 영등포구 영신로34길 19, 3
등록번호 제 312-2006-00060호
전화 02) 2636-0895
팩스 02) 2636-0896
홈페이지 www.lancom.co.kr

ISBN 979-11-92199-38-2   13740

행복한 왕자 外

THE HAPPY PRINCE
AND OTHER TALES

오스카 와일드 지음

Lan Com
Language & Communication

CONTENTS

행복한 왕자

The Happy Prince

High above the city, on a tall column, stood the statue of the Happy Prince. He was gilded all over with thin leaves of fine gold, for eyes he had two bright sapphires, and a large red ruby glowed on his sword-hilt.

He was very much admired indeed.

"He is as beautiful as a weathercock," remarked one of the Town Councillors who wished to gain a reputation for having artistic tastes; "only not quite so useful," he added, fearing lest people should think him unpractical, which he really was not.

"Why can't you be like the Happy Prince?"
~처럼
asked a sensible mother of her little boy who
분별[양식] 있는, 합리적인
was crying for the moon. "The Happy Prince
~해 달라고 울다
never dreams of crying for anything."

"I am glad there is some one in the world
기쁜, 반가운, 고마운
who is quite happy," muttered a disappointed
아주, 꽤, 상당히   중얼거리다, 투덜거리다   실망한, 낙담한
man as he gazed at the wonderful statue.
응시하다   놀라운, 훌륭한   조각상

"He looks just like an angel," said the Char-
천사   자선[구호] 단체
ity Children as they came out of the cathedral in
대성당
their bright scarlet cloaks and their clean white
주홍색   망토   깨끗한   하얀색
pinafores.
점퍼스커트, 긴 앞치마

"How do you know?" said the Mathematical
수학(상)의, 수리적(數理的)인
Master, "you have never seen one."
대가, 주인, 숙달자

"Ah! but we have, in our dreams," answered
꿈   대답하다
the children; and the Mathematical Master

frowned and looked very severe, for he did not
얼굴[눈살]을 찌푸리다[찡그리다]   극심한, 심각한
approve of children dreaming.
찬성하다, 괜찮다고 생각하다

One night there flew over the city a little
밤   날다(fly의 과거)   도시
Swallow. His friends had gone away to Egypt six
제비   친구   이집트   6주 전에
weeks before, but he had stayed behind, for he
남다, 머물다   ~뒤에
was in love with the most beautiful Reed.
~와 사랑에 빠지다   갈대

9

He had met her early in the spring as he was
이른, 빠른, 조기의 봄

flying down the river after a big yellow moth,
강 노란 나방

and had been so attracted by her slender waist
마음을 끌다 날씬한, 호리호리한 허리

that he had stopped to talk to her.
~에게 말을 걸다

"Shall I love you?" said the Swallow, who
제비

liked to come to the point at once, and the Reed
요점에 들어가다, 핵심을 찌르다 즉시, 당장, 바로

made him a low bow.
깍듯이 인사하다, 공손히 절하다

So he flew round and round her, touching
~ 주위를 뱅글뱅글 돌다 손 대다, 닿다

the water with his wings, and making silver
물 날개 은빛

ripples. This was his courtship, and it lasted all
잔물결, 파문 구애, 관심 끌기, 환심 사기 지속되다, 계속되다

through the summer.
여름 내내

"It is a ridiculous attachment," twittered the
웃기는, 말도 안 되는 애착 지저귀다[짹짹거리다]

other Swallows; "she has no money, and far too
돈

many relations"; and indeed the river was quite
친척 실제로, 정말로 강 꽤, 상당히

full of Reeds. Then, when the autumn came they
가을

all flew away.
멀리 날아가버리다

After they had gone he felt lonely, and began
외로운, 쓸쓸한

to tire of his lady- love.
싫증난, 지친

"She has no conversation," he said, "and I
대화

am afraid that she is a coquette, for she is always
요부 (=flirt) 늘, 언제나

flirting with the wind."
추파를 던지다, 시시덕거리다

And certainly, whenever the wind blew, the
틀림없이, 분명히 (= definitely)   불다
Reed made the most graceful curtseys.
우아한   절

"I admit that she is domestic," he continued,
인정[시인]하다 (= confess)   국내의, 가정(용)의, 집안의   계속하다
"but I love travelling, and my wife, consequently,
여행 다니기   그 결과, 따라서
should love travelling also."
역시, 또한

"Will you come away with me?" he said fi-
~와 함께 멀리 떠나다
nally to her; but the Reed shook her head, she
흔들다(shake의 과거, 과거분사)
was so attached to her home.
애착을 가진

"You have been trifling with me," he cried. "I
~을 우습게[하찮게] 보다, ~을 놀리다
am off to the Pyramids. Good-bye!"

And he flew away.
날아가버리다
All day long he flew, and at night-time he ar-
하루 종일   닿다, 도착하다
rived at the city.

"Where shall I put up?" he said; "I hope the
(살거나 지낼) 공간을 제공하다, 수용하다
town has made preparations."
준비, 대비
Then he saw the statue on the tall column.
조각상   원기둥, 원주
"I will put up there," he cried; "it is a fine
position, with plenty of fresh air."
위치, 자리   많은, 다량의   신선한, 상쾌한
So he alighted just between the feet of the
내려 앉다   ~사이에   발(FOOT의 복수)
Happy Prince.

11

"I have a golden bedroom," he said softly to himself as he looked round, and he prepared to go to sleep; but just as he was putting his head under his wing a large drop of water fell on him.

"What a curious thing!" he cried; "there is not a single cloud in the sky, the stars are quite clear and bright, and yet it is raining. The climate in the north of Europe is really dreadful. The Reed used to like the rain, but that was merely her selfishness."

Then another drop fell.

"What is the use of a statue if it cannot keep the rain off?" he said; "I must look for a good chimney-pot," and he determined to fly away.

But before he had opened his wings, a third drop fell, and he looked up, and saw--Ah! what did he see? The eyes of the Happy Prince were filled with tears, and tears were running down his golden cheeks. His face was so beautiful in the moonlight that the little Swallow was filled with pity.

"Who are you?" he said.

"I am the Happy Prince."

"Why are you weeping then?" asked the
Swallow; "you have quite drenched me."

"When I was alive and had a human heart,"
answered the statue, "I did not know what tears
were, for I lived in the Palace of Sans- Souci,
where sorrow is not allowed to enter. In the
daytime I played with my companions in the
garden, and in the evening I led the dance in the
Great Hall. Round the garden ran a very lofty
wall, but I never cared to ask what lay beyond it,
everything about me was so beautiful. My courtiers called me the Happy Prince, and happy indeed I was, if pleasure be happiness. So I lived,
and so I died. And now that I am dead they have
set me up here so high that I can see all the ugli-
ness and all the misery of my city, and though
my heart is made of lead yet I cannot chose but
weep."

"What! is he not solid gold?" said the Swallow to himself. He was too polite to make any personal remarks out loud.

"Far away," continued the statue in a low musical voice, "far away in a little street there is a poor house. One of the windows is open, and through it I can see a woman seated at a table. Her face is thin and worn, and she has coarse, red hands, all pricked by the needle, for she is a seamstress. She is embroidering passion-flowers on a satin gown for the loveliest of the Queen's maids-of-honour to wear at the next Court-ball. In a bed in the corner of the room her little boy is lying ill. He has a fever, and is asking for oranges. His mother has nothing to give him but river water, so he is crying. Swallow, Swallow, little Swallow, will you not bring her the ruby out of my sword-hilt? My feet are fastened to this pedestal and I cannot move."

"I am waited for in Egypt," said the Swallow. "My friends are flying up and down the Nile,

and talking to the large lotus- flowers. Soon they
will go to sleep in the tomb of the great King.
The King is there himself in his painted coffin.
He is wrapped in yellow linen, and embalmed
with spices. Round his neck is a chain of pale
green jade, and his hands are like withered
leaves."

"Swallow, Swallow, little Swallow," said the
Prince, "will you not stay with me for one night,
and be my messenger? The boy is so thirsty, and
the mother so sad."

"I don't think I like boys," answered the
Swallow. "Last summer, when I was staying on
the river, there were two rude boys, the miller's
sons, who were always throwing stones at me.
They never hit me, of course; we swallows fly far
too well for that, and besides, I come of a family
famous for its agility; but still, it was a mark of
disrespect."

But the Happy Prince looked so sad that the
little Swallow was sorry.

"It is very cold here," he said; "but I will stay
추운, 쌀쌀한
with you for one night, and be your messenger."
메신저, 사절, 심부름꾼
"Thank you, little Swallow," said the Prince.

So the Swallow picked out the great ruby
뽑아내다
from the Prince's sword, and flew away with it
검, 칼
in his beak over the roofs of the town.
(새의) 부리 (= bill)   지붕
He passed by the cathedral tower, where the
지나가다   대성당   탑
white marble angels were sculptured. He passed
대리석   천사   조각된, 조각품의
by the palace and heard the sound of dancing.
궁전   듣다   소리
A beautiful girl came out on the balcony with
발코니
her lover.

"How wonderful the stars are," he said to
놀라운, 아름다운   별
her, "and how wonderful is the power of love!"
힘, 권력
"I hope my dress will be ready in time for
바라다, 소망하다   때 맞춰, 정시에
the State-ball," she answered; "I have ordered
(궁중의) 대무도회.   주문하다
passion-flowers to be embroidered on it; but the
수놓아진
seamstresses are so lazy."
(여자) 재봉사, 침모   게으른, 나태한

He passed over the river, and saw the lanterns hanging to the masts of the ships. He passed over the Ghetto, and saw the old Jews bargaining with each other, and weighing out money in copper scales.

At last he came to the poor house and looked in. The boy was tossing feverishly on his bed, and the mother had fallen asleep, she was so tired. In he hopped, and laid the great ruby on the table beside the woman's thimble. Then he flew gently round the bed, fanning the boy's forehead with his wings.

"How cool I feel," said the boy, "I must be getting better"; and he sank into a delicious slumber.

Then the Swallow flew back to the Happy Prince, and told him what he had done.

"It is curious," he remarked, "but I feel quite warm now, although it is so cold."

"That is because you have done a good action," said the Prince.

And the little Swallow began to think, and
시작하다   생각하다
then he fell asleep. Thinking always made him
잠들다   늘, 항상, 언제나
sleepy.
졸린, 잠이 오는

When day broke he flew down to the river
날이 밝다
and had a bath.
목욕하다

"What a remarkable phenomenon," said the
주목할 만한[아주 놀라운] 현상
Professor of Ornithology as he was passing over
교수   조류학
the bridge. "A swallow in winter!"
다리   제비   겨울

And he wrote a long letter about it to the lo-
긴 편지   ~에 대하여   지역 신문
cal newspaper. Every one quoted it, it was full of
인용하다   ~로 가득 차다
so many words that they could not understand.
말, 단어   이해하다, 알다

"To-night I go to Egypt," said the Swallow,

and he was in high spirits at the prospect. He
기세가 등등해지다, 기운이 넘치다   예상, 전망
visited all the public monuments, and sat a long
방문하다   대중을 위한, 공공의 기념물[건축물]
time on top of the church steeple. Wherever he
(교회의) 첨탑
went the Sparrows chirruped, and said to each
참새   짹짹거리다   서로
other, "What a distinguished stranger!" so he
기품 있는, 위엄 있는
enjoyed himself very much. When the moon
즐기다, 누리다, 즐거워하다   달
rose he flew back to the Happy Prince.
떠오르다

"Have you any commissions for Egypt?" he
의뢰, 주문
cried; "I am just starting."

"Swallow, Swallow, little Swallow," said the
Prince, "will you not stay with me one night longer?"

"I am waited for in Egypt," answered the
Swallow. "To-morrow my friends will fly up to
the Second Cataract. The river-horse couches
there among the bulrushes, and on a great gran-
ite throne sits the God Memnon. All night long
he watches the stars, and when the morning star
shines he utters one cry of joy, and then he is silent. At noon the yellow lions come down to the
water's edge to drink. They have eyes like green
beryls, and their roar is louder than the roar of
the cataract.

"Swallow, Swallow, little Swallow," said the
Prince, "far away across the city I see a young
man in a garret. He is leaning over a desk covered with papers, and in a tumbler by his side
there is a bunch of withered violets. His hair is
brown and crisp, and his lips are red as a pome-
granate, and he has large and dreamy eyes. He

is trying to finish a play for the Director of the
마치다, 끝내다   감독
Theatre, but he is too cold to write any more.
극장   추운
There is no fire in the grate, and hunger has
                      (난로 안의 연료를 받치는) 쇠살대
made him faint."
      실신[기절/졸도]하다

"I will wait with you one night longer," said

the Swallow, who really had a good heart. "Shall
                      정말로   착한, 선한
I take him another ruby?"

"Alas! I have no ruby now," said the Prince;
이런, 맙소사
"my eyes are all that I have left. They are made
                                남다
of rare sapphires, which were brought out of In-
  진귀한, 희귀한
dia a thousand years ago. Pluck out one of them
      천 년 전에   뽑다
and take it to him. He will sell it to the jeweller,
                              팔다   보석상
and buy food and firewood, and finish his play."
    사다   음식   장작   희곡; 연극
"Dear Prince," said the Swallow, "I cannot do

that"; and he began to weep.
                      울다, 흐느끼다
"Swallow, Swallow, little Swallow," said the

Prince, "do as I command you."
                  명령하다, 지시하다 (= order)
So the Swallow plucked out the Prince's eye,
                      뽑다
and flew away to the student's garret. It was
                      학생   다락방
easy enough to get in, as there was a hole in the
쉬운, 간단한   구멍
roof.
지붕

23

Through this he darted, and came into the room. The young man had his head buried in his hands, so he did not hear the flutter of the bird's wings, and when he looked up he found the beautiful sapphire lying on the withered vio-lets.

쏜살같이[획] 달리다[움직이다] · ~속에 파묻다 · 날개의 파닥거림 · 발견하다 · 아름다운 · 사파이어 · 시든, 말라 죽은

"I am beginning to be appreciated," he cried; "this is from some great admirer. Now I can fin-ish my play," and he looked quite happy.

진가를 알아보다[인정하다] · 찬미하는 사람, 팬

The next day the Swallow flew down to the harbour. He sat on the mast of a large vessel and watched the sailors hauling big chests out of the hold with ropes.

항구, 항만 · 돛대 · (대형) 선박[배] · 선원, 뱃사람 · (아주 힘들여) 끌다 · (나무로 만든) 궤[상자]

"Heave a-hoy!" they shouted as each chest came up. "I am going to Egypt!" cried the Swal-low, but nobody minded, and when the moon rose he flew back to the Happy Prince.

(아주 무거운 것을 힘껏) 들어올리다 · 고함치다, 소리치다 · 아무도 신경 쓰지 않다

"I am come to bid you good-bye," he cried. "Swallow, Swallow, little Swallow," said the Prince, "will you not stay with me one night lon-ger?"

(인사를) 하다, (작별을) 고하다

"It is winter," answered the Swallow, "and
겨울
the chill snow will soon be here. In Egypt the
아주 차가운, 오싹한
sun is warm on the green palm-trees, and the
따뜻한   야자나무
crocodiles lie in the mud and look lazily about
악어   진흙   한가하게, 게으르게
them. My companions are building a nest in
친구, 동료   짓다, 건축하다   둥지
the Temple of Baalbec, and the pink and white
신전, 사원   분홍   하얀색
doves are watching them, and cooing to each
비둘기   지켜보다   구구 하고 울다
other. Dear Prince, I must leave you, but I will
떠나다
never forget you, and next spring I will bring
잊다   내년 좀   가져오다
you back two beautiful jewels in place of those
보석
you have given away. The ruby shall be redder
더 빨간
than a red rose, and the sapphire shall be as
장미
blue as the great sea."
파란, 푸른   바다
     "In the square below," said the Happy
광장   ~아래에
Prince, "there stands a little match-girl. She has
성냥팔이 소녀
let her matches fall in the gutter, and they are all
성냥   (도로의) 배수로
spoiled. Her father will beat her if she does not
망치다, 버려 놓다, 못쓰게 만들다   때리다
bring home some money, and she is crying. She
돈
has no shoes or stockings, and her little head is
신발   양말
bare. Pluck out my other eye, and give it to her,
벌거벗은, 헐벗은
and her father will not beat her."

"I will stay with you one night longer," said the Swallow, "but I cannot pluck out your eye. You would be quite blind then."

뽑다
눈이 먼, 맹인인

"Swallow, Swallow, little Swallow," said the Prince, "do as I command you."

명령하다, 지시하다

So he plucked out the Prince's other eye, and darted down with it. He swooped past the match-girl, and slipped the jewel into the palm of her hand.

쏜살같이 날아가다
급강하하다
미끄러뜨리다
보석
손바닥

"What a lovely bit of glass," cried the little girl; and she ran home, laughing.

웃으면서

Then the Swallow came back to the Prince. "You are blind now," he said, "so I will stay with you always."

머물다

"No, little Swallow," said the poor Prince, "you must go away to Egypt."

가련한, 불쌍한

"I will stay with you always," said the Swallow, and he slept at the Prince's feet.

잠자다

All the next day he sat on the Prince's shoulder, and told him stories of what he had seen in strange lands.

어깨
이야기
낯선
땅, 육지, 물

He told him of the red ibises (따오기(새의 일종)), who stand in long rows on the banks (강변, 강둑) of the Nile, and catch (잡다) gold-fish (금붕어) in their beaks (부리); of the Sphinx (스핑크스), who is as old as the world itself (이 세상 만큼 나이를 먹은), and lives in the desert (사막), and knows everything (모든 것); of the merchants (상인, (특히) 무역상), who walk slowly (천천히, 느리게) by the side of their camels (낙타), and carry amber (호박) beads (염주, 구슬) in their hands; of the King of the Mountains (산) of the Moon (달), who is as black as (~만큼 검은) ebony (흑단), and worships (예배하다, 숭배하다) a large crystal; of the great green snake (뱀) that sleeps in a palm-tree (야자나무), and has twenty priests (사제, 신부, 성직자) to feed it with honey-cakes (벌꿀 케이크); and of the pygmies (피그미족) who sail over a big lake (호수) on large flat (평평한) leaves (나뭇잎), and are always at war (전쟁, 전투) with the butterflies (나비).

"Dear little Swallow," said the Prince, "you tell me of marvellous (놀라운, 믿기 어려운, 신기한) things, but more marvellous than anything is the suffering ((육체적 · 정신적) 고통, 괴로움) of men and of women. There is no Mystery (수수께끼, 미스터리) so great as Misery (고통, 비참함). Fly over my city, little Swallow, and tell me what you see there."

So the Swallow flew over the great city, and saw the rich making merry in their beautiful houses, while the beggars were sitting at the gates. He flew into dark lanes, and saw the white faces of starving children looking out listlessly at the black streets. Under the archway of a bridge two little boys were lying in one another's arms to try and keep themselves warm.

"How hungry we are!" they said.

"You must not lie here," shouted the Watch-man, and they wandered out into the rain.

Then he flew back and told the Prince what he had seen.

"I am covered with fine gold," said the Prince, "you must take it off, leaf by leaf, and give it to my poor; the living always think that gold can make them happy."

Leaf after leaf of the fine gold the Swallow picked off, till the Happy Prince looked quite dull and grey. Leaf after leaf of the fine gold he brought to the poor, and the children's faces

grew rosier, and they laughed and played games
in the street.

"We have bread now!" they cried.

Then the snow came, and after the snow
came the frost. The streets looked as if they were
made of silver, they were so bright and glisten-
ing; long icicles like crystal daggers hung down
from the eaves of the houses, everybody went
about in furs, and the little boys wore scarlet
caps and skated on the ice.

The poor little Swallow grew colder and
colder, but he would not leave the Prince, he
loved him too well. He picked up crumbs outside the baker's door when the baker was not
looking and tried to keep himself warm by flapping his wings.

But at last he knew that he was going to die.
He had just strength to fly up to the Prince's
shoulder once more.

"Good-bye, dear Prince!" he murmured, "will
you let me kiss your hand?"

"I am glad that you are going to Egypt at last, little Swallow," said the Prince, "you have stayed too long here; but you must kiss me on the lips, for I love you."

"It is not to Egypt that I am going," said the Swallow. "I am going to the House of Death. Death is the brother of Sleep, is he not?"

And he kissed the Happy Prince on the lips, and fell down dead at his feet.

At that moment a curious crack sounded inside the statue, as if something had broken. The fact is that the leaden heart had snapped right in two. It certainly was a dreadfully hard frost.

Early the next morning the Mayor was walking in the square below in company with the Town Councillors. As they passed the column he looked up at the statue: "Dear me! how shabby the Happy Prince looks!" he said.

"How shabby indeed!" cried the Town Councillors, who always agreed with the Mayor; and they went up to look at it.

30

"The ruby has fallen out of his sword, his eyes are gone, and he is golden no longer," said the Mayor in fact, "he is litttle beter than a beggar!"

"Little better than a beggar," said the Town Councillors.

"And here is actually a dead bird at his feet!" continued the Mayor. "We must really issue a proclamation that birds are not to be allowed to die here."

And the Town Clerk made a note of the suggestion. So they pulled down the statue of the Happy Prince.

"As he is no longer beautiful he is no longer useful," said the Art Professor at the University. Then they melted the statue in a furnace, and the Mayor held a meeting of the Corporation to decide what was to be done with the metal.

"We must have another statue, of course," he said, "and it shall be a statue of myself."

"Of myself," said each of the Town Councillors, and they quarrelled. When I last heard of
them they were quarrelling still.

"What a strange thing!" said the overseer
of the workmen at the foundry. "This broken
lead heart will not melt in the furnace. We must
throw it away."

So they threw it on a dust-heap where the
dead Swallow was also lying.

"Bring me the two most precious things in
the city," said God to one of His Angels; and the
Angel brought Him the leaden heart and the
dead bird.

"You have rightly chosen," said God, "for in
my garden of Paradise this little bird shall sing
for evermore, and in my city of gold the Happy
Prince shall praise me."

나이팅게일과 장미

The Nightingale and the Rose

"She said that she would dance with me if I brought her red roses," cried the young Student; "but in all my garden there is no red rose."

From her nest in the holm-oak tree the Nightingale heard him, and she looked out through the leaves, and wondered.

"No red rose in all my garden!" he cried, and his beautiful eyes filled with tears. "Ah, on what little things does happiness depend! I have read all that the wise men have written, and all the secrets of philosophy are mine, yet for want of a red rose is my life made wretched."

"Here at last is a true lover," said the Night-
마침내, 결국 / 진실한, 진정한

ingale. "Night after night have I sung of him,
노래하다

though I knew him not: night after night have
(비록) …이긴 하지만[…인데도]

I told his story to the stars, and now I see him.
이야기 / 별 / 보다, 알다

His hair is dark as the hyacinth-blossom, and
머리카락 / 검은 / 히아신스 꽃

his lips are red as the rose of his desire; but pas-
입술 / ~처럼, ~만큼 / 바라다, 원하다 / 열정

sion has made his face like pale ivory, and sor-
얼굴 / 창백한 / 상아 / 깊은 슬픔, 비탄

row has set her seal upon his brow."
도장을 찍다 / 이마 (=forehead)

"The Prince gives a ball to-morrow night,"
왕자 / 무도회를 열다

murmured the young Student, "and my love will
중얼거리다 / 젊은

be of the company. If I bring her a red rose she
손님, 함께 있는 사람들

will dance with me till dawn. If I bring her a red
~까지 / 새벽, 동틀녘

rose, I shall hold her in my arms, and she will
잡고[쥐고/들고/안고/받치고] 있다

lean her head upon my shoulder, and her hand
기대다 / 머리 / 어깨 / 손

will be clasped in mine. But there is no red rose
(꽉) 움켜쥐다[움켜잡다]

in my garden, so I shall sit lonely, and she will
외로이, 쓸쓸하게

pass me by. She will have no heed of me, and
지나치다, 지나가다 / ~에 관심을 갖다[주의를 기울이다]

my heart will break."
마음, 심장 / 깨지다, 부서지다

"Here indeed is the true lover," said the
Nightingale. "What I sing of, he suffers--what is
joy to me, to him is pain. Surely Love is a wonderful thing. It is more precious than emeralds,
and dearer than fine opals. Pearls and pome-
granates cannot buy it, nor is it set forth in the
marketplace. It may not be purchased of the
merchants, nor can it be weighed out in the bal-
ance for gold."

"The musicians will sit in their gallery,"
said the young Student, "and play upon their
stringed instruments, and my love will dance
to the sound of the harp and the violin. She
will dance so lightly that her feet will not touch
the floor, and the courtiers in their gay dresses
will throng round her. But with me she will not
dance, for I have no red rose to give her."

And he flung himself down on the grass, and
buried his face in his hands, and wept.

"Why is he weeping?" asked a little Green
Lizard, as he ran past him with his tail in the air.

"Why, indeed?" said a Butterfly, who was
fluttering about after a sunbeam.

"Why, indeed?" whispered a Daisy to his
neighbour, in a soft, low voice.

"He is weeping for a red rose," said the
Nightingale.

"For a red rose?" they cried; "how very ridiculous!"

And the little Lizard, who was something of
a cynic, laughed outright.

But the Nightingale understood the secret
of the Student's sorrow, and she sat silent in
the oak-tree, and thought about the mystery of
Love.

Suddenly she spread her brown wings
for flight, and soared into the air. She passed
through the grove like a shadow, and like a
shadow she sailed across the garden.

In the centre of the grass-plot was standing
a beautiful Rose-tree, and when she saw it she
flew over to it, and lit upon a spray.

"Give me a red rose," she cried, "and I will sing you my sweetest song."

But the Tree shook its head.
가장 달콤한 고개를 흔들다

"My roses are white," it answered; "as white as the foam of the sea, and whiter than the snow upon the mountain. But go to my brother who grows round the old sun-dial, and perhaps he will give you what you want."
대답하다 거품, 포말 (=froth) (큰) 산 형제 자라다 해시계 아마, 어쩌면 주다 원하다, 바라다

So the Nightingale flew over to the Rose-tree that was growing round the old sun-dial.

"Give me a red rose," she cried, "and I will sing you my sweetest song."

But the Tree shook its head.

"My roses are yellow," it answered; "as yel-low as the hair of the mermaiden who sits upon an amber throne, and yellower than the daffodil that blooms in the meadow before the mower comes with his scythe. But go to my brother who grows beneath the Student's window, and perhaps he will give you what you want."
노란색 머리카락 인어 아가씨 호박(색) 왕좌, 옥좌 수선화 꽃 초원, 목초지 (풀) 베는 기계 큰 낫 아래[밑]에 창문

So the Nightingale flew over to the Rose-tree
~위로 날아가다
that was growing beneath the Student's window.

"Give me a red rose," she cried, "and I will
sing you my sweetest song."

But the Tree shook its head.

"My roses are red," it answered, "as red as
장미
the feet of the dove, and redder than the great
발   비둘기
fans of coral that wave and wave in the ocean-
부채   산호   흔들다, 물결치다   대양의 커다란 동굴
cavern. But the winter has chilled my veins, and
겨울   아주 춥게 만들다 (식물의) 잎맥
the frost has nipped my buds, and the storm has
서리   할퀴고 가다[해치다] 꽃봉오리, 눈   태풍, 폭풍
broken my branches, and I shall have no roses
부수다, 깨뜨리다 가지
at all this year."

"One red rose is all I want," cried the Nightingale, "only one red rose! Is there no way by
방법
which I can get it?"
얻다
"There is a way," answered the Tree; "but it
방법   대답하다   나무
is so terrible that I dare not tell it to you."
끔찍한, 무시무시한   감히 ~하다
"Tell it to me," said the Nightingale, "I am
not afraid."
두려운, 무서운
"If you want a red rose," said the Tree, "you
must build it out of music by moonlight, and
짓다, 만들어내다   음악   달빛

40

stain it with your own heart's blood. You must
착색하다 심장의 피

sing to me with your breast against a thorn. All
노래하다 가슴 (식물의) 가시

night long you must sing to me, and the thorn

must pierce your heart, and your life-blood
뚫다, 찌르다

must flow into my veins, and become mine."
~속으로 흐르다

"Death is a great price to pay for a red rose,"
죽음 값, (치러야 할) 대가

cried the Nightingale, "and Life is very dear to
삶 소중한, 귀한

all. It is pleasant to sit in the green wood, and
즐거운, 유쾌한 숲

to watch the Sun in his chariot of gold, and the
지켜보다 (고대의 전투나 경주용) 마차[전차]

Moon in her chariot of pearl. Sweet is the scent
진주 향긋한 냄새

of the hawthorn, and sweet are the bluebells
산사나무 블루벨, 초롱꽃

that hide in the valley, and the heather that
숨다, 감추다 계곡, 골짜기 히스꽃

blows on the hill. Yet Love is better than Life,
언덕 하지만, 그러나

and what is the heart of a bird compared to the
심장 새 ~과 비교하다

heart of a man?"

So she spread her brown wings for flight,
펴다, 펼치다

and soared into the air. She swept over the gar-
솟구치다, 날아오르다 미끄러지듯 움직이다

den like a shadow, and like a shadow she sailed
그림자 나아가다

through the grove.
작은 숲

The young Student was still lying on the
여전히, 아직도
grass, where she had left him, and the tears
풀, 잔디   눈물
were not yet dry in his beautiful eyes.
마른, 건조한

"Be happy," cried the Nightingale, "be hap-

py; you shall have your red rose. I will build it
짓다, 만들어내다
out of music by moonlight, and stain it with my
음악   달빛   착색하다
own heart's-blood. All that I ask of you in return
~에 대한 보답으로
is that you will be a true lover, for Love is wiser
진정한, 진실한   더 현명한
than Philosophy, though she is wise, and might-
철학   비록 ~지만[라고 해도]   ~보다 더 힘센
ier than Power, though he is mighty. Flame-
힘, 권력   불타는 듯한 빨간색
coloured are his wings, and coloured like flame
날개
is his body. His lips are sweet as honey, and his
몸, 신체   입술   꿀
breath is like frankincense."
가슴   유향

The Student looked up from the grass, and

listened, but he could not understand what the
경청하다, 귀 기울여 듣다   이해하다, 알다
Nightingale was saying to him, for he only knew
오직, 그저
the things that are written down in books.
적혀 있는   책
But the Oak-tree understood, and felt sad,
떡갈나무   슬픔을 느끼다
for he was very fond of the little Nightingale
무척 좋아하다
who had built her nest in his branches.
둥지   나뭇가지

42

"Sing me one last song," he whispered; "I
마지막 노래 속삭이다
shall feel very lonely when you are gone."
외로운, 쓸쓸한

So the Nightingale sang to the Oak-tree, and
her voice was like water bubbling from a silver
목소리 거품이 일다 은의, 은으로 된
jar. When she had finished her song the Student
(큰) 병 마치다, 끝내다
got up, and pulled a note-book and a lead-pencil
일어나다 꺼내다 수첩, 공책 연필
out of his pocket.
주머니

"She has form," he said to himself, as he
형식, 양식, 형태
walked away through the grove--"that cannot
작은 숲
be denied to her; but has she got feeling? I am
사실이 아니라고 말하다, 부인[부정]하다 감정을 느끼다
afraid not. In fact, she is like most artists; she is
사실, 실제로 대부분의 예술가들
all style, without any sincerity. She would not
성실, 정직, 진심
sacrifice herself for others. She thinks merely of
희생하다 그저, 단순히
music, and everybody knows that the arts are
음악
selfish. Still, it must be admitted that she has
이기적인, 자기중심적인 인정하다, 시인하다
some beautiful notes in her voice. What a pity
동정, 연민
it is that they do not mean anything, or do any
뜻하다, 의미하다
practical good."
현실적인, 실질적인

And he went into his room, and lay down on
his little pallet-bed, and began to think of his
초라한 침대
love; and, after a time, he fell asleep.
잠들다

44

And when the Moon shone in the heavens
the Nightingale flew to the Rose-tree, and set
her breast against the thorn.

All night long she sang with her breast
against the thorn, and the cold crystal Moon
leaned down and listened.

All night long she sang, and the thorn went
deeper and deeper into her breast, and her life-
blood ebbed away from her.

She sang first of the birth of love in the heart
of a boy and a girl. And on the top-most spray
of the Rose-tree there blossomed a marvellous
rose, petal following petal, as song followed
song.

Pale was it, at first, as the mist that hangs
over the river--pale as the feet of the morning,
and silver as the wings of the dawn.
As the shadow of a rose in a mirror of silver,
as the shadow of a rose in a water-pool, so was
the rose that blossomed on the topmost spray of
the Tree.

But the Tree cried to the Nightingale to press
누르다
closer against the thorn.
더 가까이
"Press closer, little Nightingale," cried the
Tree, "or the Day will come before the rose is
날이 밝다   ~전에
finished."

So the Nightingale pressed closer against the
thorn, and louder and louder grew her song, for
더욱 더 크게
she sang of the birth of passion in the soul of a
격정, 열정   영혼, 정신
man and a maid.

And a delicate flush of pink came into the
섬세한, 우아한   홍조, 붉은 빛
leaves of the rose, like the flush in the face of the
잎사귀
bridegroom when he kisses the lips of the bride.
신랑   신부
But the thorn had not yet reached her heart,
닿다, 이르다
so the rose's heart remained white, for only a
남아 있다
Nightingale's heart's-blood can crimson the
진홍색의
heart of a rose.

And the Tree cried to the Nightingale to
소리치다, 외치다
press closer against the thorn.

"Press closer, little Nightingale," cried the
Tree, "or the Day will come before the rose is
finished."

So the Nightingale pressed closer against the thorn, and the thorn touched her heart, and a fierce pang of pain shot through her.

Bitter, bitter was the pain, and wilder and wilder grew her song, for she sang of the Love that is perfected by Death, of the Love that dies not in the tomb.

And the marvellous rose became crimson, like the rose of the eastern sky. Crimson was the girdle of petals, and crimson as a ruby was the heart.

But the Nightingale's voice grew fainter, and her little wings began to beat, and a film came over her eyes. Fainter and fainter grew her song, and she felt something choking her in her throat.

Then she gave one last burst of music. The white Moon heard it, and she forgot the dawn, and lingered on in the sky. The red rose heard it, and it trembled all over with ecstasy, and opened its petals to the cold morning air.

Echo (메아리) bore it to her purple (보랏빛의) cavern (동굴) in the hills (언덕),
and woke (깨우다) the sleeping shepherds (양치기) from their
dreams. It floated (떠[흘러]가다[떠돌다]) through the reeds (갈대) of the river (강),
and they carried (나르다, 운반하다) its message (전갈, 메시지) to the sea.

"Look, look!" cried the Tree, "the rose is
finished (마치다, 완성하다) now"; but the Nightingale made no answer, for she was lying dead (죽은) in the long grass (풀, 잔디),
with the thorn in her heart.

And at noon (정오에, 낮 12시에) the Student opened (열다) his window (창문)
and looked out.

"Why, what a wonderful (놀라운, 훌륭한) piece of luck (행운)!" he
cried; "here is a red rose! I have never seen any
rose like it in all my life. It is so beautiful that
I am sure it has a long (긴) Latin name (라틴어 이름)"; and he
leaned down (몸을 숙이다) and plucked (따다, 꺾다) it.

Then he put on (쓰다, 입다, 끼다) his hat (모자), and ran up (달려가다) to the
Professor's (교수) house with the rose in his hand.

The daughter (딸) of the Professor was sitting in
the doorway (출입구, 현관문) winding ((실 등을) 감다) blue silk on a reel (릴, 얼레), and her
little dog was lying at her feet.

48

"You said that you would dance with me if
I brought you a red rose," cried the Student.
"Here is the reddest rose in all the world. You
will wear it to-night next your heart, and as we
dance together it will tell you how I love you."

But the girl frowned.

"I am afraid it will not go with my dress,"
she answered; "and, besides, the Chamberlain's
nephew has sent me some real jewels, and everybody knows that jewels cost far more than
flowers."

"Well, upon my word, you are very ungrateful," said the Student angrily; and he threw the
rose into the street, where it fell into the gutter,
and a cart-wheel went over it.

"Ungrateful!" said the girl. "I tell you what,
you are very rude; and, after all, who are you?
Only a Student. Why, I don't believe you have
even got silver buckles to your shoes as the
Chamberlain's nephew has"; and she got up
from her chair and went into the house.

"What a silly thing Love is," said the Student as he walked away. "It is not half as useful as Logic, for it does not prove anything, and it is always telling one of things that are not going to happen, and making one believe things that are not true. In fact, it is quite unpractical, and, as in this age to be practical is everything, I shall go back to Philosophy and study Metaphysics."

So he returned to his room and pulled out a great dusty book, and began to read.

이기적인 거인

The Selfish Giant

Every afternoon, as they were coming from school, the children used to go and play in the Giant's garden.

It was a large lovely garden, with soft green grass. Here and there over the grass stood beautiful flowers like stars, and there were twelve peach-trees that in the spring-time broke out into delicate blossoms of pink and pearl, and in the autumn bore rich fruit. The birds sat on the trees and sang so sweetly that the children used to stop their games in order to listen to them.

"How happy we are here!" they cried to each other.

One day the Giant came back. He had been to visit his friend the Cornish ogre, and had stayed with him for seven years.

거인 / 돌아오다 / 방문하다 / 친구 / 콘월의 / 사람을 잡아먹는 거인 / 묵다, 머물다 / 7년 동안

After the seven years were over he had said all that he had to say, for his conversation was limited, and he determined to return to his own castle. When he arrived he saw the children playing in the garden.

~뒤에 / 끝나다, 파하다 / 대화 / 한계에 다다르다 / 결정하다, 결심하다 / 돌아오다, 귀환하다 / 성 / 도착하다

"What are you doing here?" he cried in a very gruff voice, and the children ran away.

외치다 / 걸걸한, 거친 / 달아나다, 도망치다

"My own garden is my own garden," said the Giant; "any one can understand that, and I will allow nobody to play in it but myself."

… 자신의[…의] / 이해하다 / 허락하다, 용납하다

So he built a high wall all round it, and put up a notice-board.

짓다, 세우다 / 벽, 담 / 사방을 빙 둘러 / 게시판, 고시판, 공고판

TRESPASSERS
무단출입[침입]자
WILL BE
PROSECUTED
기소[고발/소추]하다

He was a very selfish Giant.

이기적인, 자기중심적인

The poor children had now nowhere to play.
불쌍한, 가엾은

They tried to play on the road, but the road was
시도하다   길, 도로

very dusty and full of hard stones, and they did
먼지투성이인   ~으로 가득한   단단한 돌덩이

not like it.

They used to wander round the high wall
배회하다, 거닐다   ~주위를

when their lessons were over, and talk about the
수업   끝나다, 파하다   ~에 대해 이야기를 나누다

beautiful garden inside.
내부, 안쪽

"How happy we were there," they said to

each other.

Then the Spring came, and all over the coun-
봄   곳곳에, 온 데, ~전체에

try there were little blossoms and little birds.
꽃   새

Only in the garden of the Selfish Giant it was
오직, 단지

still winter. The birds did not care to sing in it as
아직(도) (계속해서)   새

there were no children, and the trees forgot to
잊다

blossom.
꽃을 피우다

Once a beautiful flower put its head out from
한 번, (과거) 언젠가   머리를 내밀다

the grass, but when it saw the notice-board it
풀, 잔디   게시판, 공보판

was so sorry for the children that it slipped back
안된, 안쓰러운, 애석한   미끄러지다

into the ground again, and went off to sleep.
땅, 흙   다시

The only people who were pleased were the
사람   기쁜, 즐거운

Snow and the Frost.

"Spring has forgotten this garden," they
cried, "so we will live here all the year round."

The Snow covered up the grass with her
great white cloak, and the Frost painted all the
trees silver. Then they invited the North Wind
to stay with them, and he came.

He was wrapped in furs, and he roared all
day about the garden, and blew the chimney-
pots down.

"This is a delightful spot," he said, "we must
ask the Hail on a visit."

So the Hail came. Every day for three hours
he rattled on the roof of the castle till he broke
most of the slates, and then he ran round and
round the garden as fast as he could go. He was
dressed in grey, and his breath was like ice.

"I cannot understand why the Spring is so
late in coming," said the Selfish Giant, as he sat
at the window and looked out at his cold white
garden; "I hope there will be a change in the
weather."

55

But the Spring never came, nor the Summer.
The Autumn gave golden fruit to every garden, but to the Giant's garden she gave none.

"He is too selfish," she said. So it was always Winter there, and the North Wind, and the Hail, and the Frost, and the Snow danced about through the trees.

One morning the Giant was lying awake in bed when he heard some lovely music. It sounded so sweet to his ears that he thought it must be the King's musicians passing by. It was really only a little linnet singing outside his window, but it was so long since he had heard a bird sing in his garden that it seemed to him to be the most beautiful music in the world. Then the Hail stopped dancing over his head, and the North Wind ceased roaring, and a delicious perfume came to him through the open casement.

"I believe the Spring has come at last," said the Giant; and he jumped out of bed and looked out.

What did he see?

He saw a most wonderful sight. Through
a little hole in the wall the children had crept
in, and they were sitting in the branches of the
trees. In every tree that he could see there was
a little child. And the trees were so glad to have
the children back again that they had covered
themselves with blossoms, and were waving
their arms gently above the children's heads.

The birds were flying about and twittering
with delight, and the flowers were looking up
through the green grass and laughing.

It was a lovely scene, only in one corner it
was still winter. It was the farthest corner of the
garden, and in it was standing a little boy. He
was so small that he could not reach up to the
branches of the tree, and he was wandering all
round it, crying bitterly.

The poor tree was still quite covered with
frost and snow, and the North Wind was blowing and roaring above it.

57

"Climb up! little boy," said the Tree, and it
bent its branches down as low as it could; but
the boy was too tiny.

And the Giant's heart melted as he looked
out.

"How selfish I have been!" he said; "now
I know why the Spring would not come here.
I will put that poor little boy on the top of the
tree, and then I will knock down the wall, and
my garden shall be the children's playground for
ever and ever."

He was really very sorry for what he had
done.

So he crept downstairs and opened the front
door quite softly, and went out into the garden.
But when the children saw him they were so
frightened that they all ran away, and the garden became winter again.

Only the little boy did not run, for his eyes
were so full of tears that he did not see the Giant
coming.

And the Giant stole up behind him and took
살며시 움직이다 (=creep) (STEAL의 과거)
him gently in his hand, and put him up into the
다정하게
tree. And the tree broke at once into blossom,
즉시, 당장, 곧바로
and the birds came and sang on it, and the little
boy stretched out his two arms and flung them
쭉 뻗다   팔   fling의 과거, 과거분사
round the Giant's neck, and kissed him.
목

And the other children, when they saw that
the Giant was not wicked any longer, came run-
사악한, 못된
ning back, and with them came the Spring.

"It is your garden now, little children," said
the Giant, and he took a great axe and knocked
도끼   부수다, 철거하다
down the wall. And when the people were going
사람들
to market at twelve o'clock they found the Giant
시장   12시
playing with the children in the most beautiful
garden they had ever seen.

All day long they played, and in the evening
저녁
they came to the Giant to bid him good-bye.
작별 인사를 하다
"But where is your little companion?" he
친구, 동료
said: "the boy I put into the tree."

The Giant loved him the best because he had
최고, 최상   왜냐하면, ~때문에
kissed him.

"We don't know," answered the children; "he has gone away."

"You must tell him to be sure and come here to-morrow," said the Giant.

But the children said that they did not know where he lived, and had never seen him before; and the Giant felt very sad.

Every afternoon, when school was over, the children came and played with the Giant. But the little boy whom the Giant loved was never seen again.

The Giant was very kind to all the children, yet he longed for his first little friend, and often spoke of him.

"How I would like to see him!" he used to say.

Years went over, and the Giant grew very old and feeble. He could not play about any more, so he sat in a huge armchair, and watched the children at their games, and admired his garden.

"I have many beautiful flowers," he said;
"but the children are the most beautiful flowers
of all."

One winter morning he looked out of his
window as he was dressing. He did not hate the
Winter now, for he knew that it was merely the
Spring asleep, and that the flowers were resting.
Suddenly he rubbed his eyes in wonder, and
looked and looked. It certainly was a marvellous
sight. In the farthest corner of the garden was a
tree quite covered with lovely white blossoms.
Its branches were all golden, and silver fruit
hung down from them, and underneath it stood
the little boy he had loved.

Downstairs ran the Giant in great joy, and
out into the garden. He hastened across the
grass, and came near to the child. And when he
came quite close his face grew red with anger,
and he said, "Who hath dared to wound thee?"

For on the palms of the child's hands were
the prints of two nails, and the prints of two
nails were on the little feet.

"Who hath dared to wound thee?" cried the
Giant; "tell me, that I may take my big sword
and slay him."

"Nay!" answered the child; "but these are the
wounds of Love."

"Who art thou?" said the Giant, and a
strange awe fell on him, and he knelt before the
little child.

And the child smiled on the Giant, and said
to him, "You let me play once in your garden,
to-day you shall come with me to my garden,
which is Paradise."

And when the children ran in that afternoon,
they found the Giant lying dead under the tree,
all covered with white blossoms.

헌신적인 친구

The Devoted Friend

One morning the old Water-rat put his
head out of his hole. He had bright beady
eyes and stiff grey whiskers and his tail was like
a long bit of black india-rubber.

The little ducks were swimming about in the
pond, looking just like a lot of yellow canaries,
and their mother, who was pure white with real
red legs, was trying to teach them how to stand
on their heads in the water.

"You will never be in the best society unless
you can stand on your heads," she kept saying to
them; and every now and then she showed them
how it was done.

But the little ducks paid no attention to her.
오리　　　　관심을 갖지 않다, 주의를 기울이지 않다

They were so young that they did not know what
너무 어려서　　　　　　　　　알다

an advantage it is to be in society at all.
유리한 점, 이점, 장점　　　　　　전혀, 조금도 (…아니다)

"What disobedient children!" cried the old
반항하는, 거역하는, 말 안 듣는

Water-rat; "they really deserve to be drowned."
…을 (당)해야 마땅하다　물에 빠져 죽다, 익사하다

"Nothing of the kind," answered the Duck,
결코 그런 것이 아니다, 전혀 그렇지 않다, 얼토당토 않다

"every one must make a beginning, and parents
시작　　　　　　부모

cannot be too patient."
참을성[인내심] 있는

"Ah! I know nothing about the feelings of
아무것도[단 하나도] (…아니다/없다)　감정, 느낌

parents," said the Water- rat; "I am not a fam-
부모　　　　　　　　　　　　　　가정이 있는

ily man. In fact, I have never been married, and
사실, 실제로　　　　　　　결혼하다

I never intend to be. Love is all very well in its
의도[작정]하다, (…하려고) 생각하다　　　　　그 나름대로

way, but friendship is much higher. Indeed, I
우정, 친선, 교우 관계　　　　더 높은, 더 숭고한

know of nothing in the world that is either no-
더 고귀한, 숭고한

bler or rarer than a devoted friendship."
더 드문, 더 진귀한　헌신적인

"And what, pray, is your idea of the duties of
발상, 견해, 신념　의무

a devoted friend?" asked a Green Linnet, who
홍방울새

was sitting in a willow-tree hard by, and had
버드나무　　　매우 가까운

overheard the conversation.
우연히 듣다　　대화

"Yes, that is just what I want to know," said the Duck; and she swam away to the end of the pond, and stood upon her head, in order to give her children a good example.

"What a silly question!" cried the Water-rat. "I should expect my devoted friend to be devoted to me, of course."

"And what would you do in return?" said the little bird, swinging upon a silver spray, and flapping his tiny wings.

"I don't understand you," answered the Water-rat.

"Let me tell you a story on the subject," said the Linnet.

"Is the story about me?" asked the Water-rat. "If so, I will listen to it, for I am extremely fond of fiction."

"It is applicable to you," answered the Linnet; and he flew down, and alighting upon the bank, he told the story of The Devoted Friend.

"Once upon a time," said the Linnet, "there was an honest little fellow named Hans."

"Was he very distinguished?" asked the Water-rat.

"No," answered the Linnet, "I don't think he was distinguished at all, except for his kind heart, and his funny round good-humoured face. He lived in a tiny cottage all by himself, and every day he worked in his garden. In all the country-side there was no garden so lovely as his.

"Sweet-william grew there, and Gilly-flowers, and Shepherds'-purses, and Fair-maids of France. There were damask Roses, and yellow Roses, lilac Crocuses, and gold, purple Violets and white.

"Columbine and Ladysmock, Marjoram and Wild Basil, the Cowslip and the Flower-de-luce, the Daffodil and the Clove-Pink bloomed or blossomed in their proper order as the months went by, one flower taking another flower's place, so that there were always beautiful things [always: 늘, 항상 / beautiful: 아름다운] to look at, and pleasant odours to smell. [pleasant: 쾌적한, 기분 좋은 / odours: 냄새, 향기 / smell: 냄새[향]가 나다]

"Little Hans had a great many friends, but [a great many: 아주 많은, 엄청나게 많은] the most devoted friend of all was big Hugh the [most: 가장 / devoted: 헌신적인] Miller. Indeed, so devoted was the rich Miller to [Miller: 방앗간[제분소] 주인[일꾼] / rich: 부유한] little Hans, that be would never go by his gar- [go by: 지나가다] den without leaning over the wall and plucking [without: ~없이 / leaning: 몸을 구부리다 / wall: 벽, 담 / plucking: (꽃을) 따다[꺾다]] a large nosegay, or a handful of sweet herbs, or [nosegay: 꽃다발 / a handful of: 한 움큼, 한 주먹 가득 / herbs: 허브, 약초, 향초] filling his pockets with plums and cherries if it [filling: ~으로 채우다 / pockets: 주머니 / plums: 자두 / cherries: 체리] was the fruit season. [fruit: 과일, 열매 / season: 철, 시즌]

"'Real friends should have everything in [Real: 진짜의, 현실적인, 실제의 / everything: 모든 것 / in common: 공동으로] common,' the Miller used to say, and little Hans [used to: ~하곤 했다] nodded and smiled, and felt very proud of hav- [nodded: 고개를 끄덕이다 / smiled: 미소를 짓다 / felt: 느끼다 / proud: 자랑스러운] ing a friend with such noble ideas. [noble: 고귀한[숭고한] 생각[이념, 발상]]

"Sometimes, indeed, the neighbours thought [Sometimes: 가끔, 때때로 / indeed: 정말, 참으로 / neighbours: 이웃(사람들)] it strange that the rich Miller never gave little [strange: 이상한, 기이한 / rich: 부유한, 부자인 / gave: 주다] Hans anything in return, though he had a [in return: 보답으로, 보상으로 / though: ~하면서도, ~인데도] hundred sacks of flour stored away in his mill, [sacks: 포대(布袋), 자루 / flour: 밀가루 / stored: 저장[보관]하다] and six milch cows, and a large flock of woolly [milch cows: 젖소 / flock: 떼, 무리 / woolly: 털북숭이의] sheep; but Hans never troubled his head about [sheep: 양 / troubled his head: 괴롭히다, 애 먹이다] these things, and nothing gave him greater plea-

sure than to listen to all the wonderful things
the Miller used to say about the unselfishness of
true friendship.

"So little Hans worked away in his garden.
During the spring, the summer, and the autumn
he was very happy, but when the winter came,
and he had no fruit or flowers to bring to the
market, he suffered a good deal from cold and
hunger, and often had to go to bed without any
supper but a few dried pears or some hard nuts.
In the winter, also, he was extremely lonely, as
the Miller never came to see him then.

"'There is no good in my going to see little
Hans as long as the snow lasts,' the Miller used
to say to his wife, 'for when people are in trouble
they should be left alone, and not be bothered
by visitors. That at least is my idea about friendship, and I am sure I am right. So I shall wait till
the spring comes, and then I shall pay him a visit, and he will be able to give me a large basket
of primroses and that will make him so happy.'

"'You are certainly very thoughtful about
분명히, 틀림없이 　　　　　사려 깊은, 심사숙고하는
others,' answered the Wife, as she sat in her
대답하다
comfortable armchair by the big pinewood fire;
편(안)한, 쾌적한 　　안락의자 　　　　　소나무 재목
'very thoughtful indeed. It is quite a treat to hear
정말로, 실제로 　　꽤, 상당히 　대접, 한턱
you talk about friendship. I am sure the clergy-
~에 대해 이야기하다 　　　　　　　　　성직자
man himself could not say such beautiful things
as you do, though he does live in a three-storied
비록 ~라 해도 　　　　　3층집
house, and wear a gold ring on his little finger.'
금반지를 끼다 　　　　　　　손가락
"'But could we not ask little Hans up here?'
~을 ~로 초대하다
said the Miller's youngest son. 'If poor Hans is
막내아들 　　　　불쌍한, 가엾은
in trouble I will give him half my porridge, and
곤경에 처하여, 난처하여 　　　　　포리지(죽의 일종)
show him my white rabbits.'
토끼
"'What a silly boy you are'! cried the Miller; 'I
어리석은, 바보 같은 (= foolish)
really don't know what is the use of sending you
정말로, 실제로 　　　　~의 소용 　보내는 것
to school. You seem not to learn anything. Why,
학교 　　　　　　　　　배우다
if little Hans came up here, and saw our warm
따뜻한
fire, and our good supper, and our great cask
훌륭한 식사 　　　　　커다란 통(포도주 통)
of red wine, he might get envious, and envy is a
붉은 포도주, 레드 와인 　　　부러워하는, 선망하는
most terrible thing, and would spoil anybody's
가장 　끔찍한, 무서운 　　　　망치다, 버려 놓다
nature. I certainly will not allow Hans' nature
천성, 성품 　　　　　　허락하다, 용납하다
to be spoiled. I am his best friend, and I will

73

always watch over him, and see that he is not
led into any temptations. Besides, if Hans came
here, he might ask me to let him have some
flour on credit, and that I could not do. Flour
is one thing, and friendship is another, and
they should not be confused. Why, the words
are spelt differently, and mean quite different
things. Everybody can see that.'

'"How well you talk'! said the Miller's Wife,
pouring herself out a large glass of warm ale;
'really I feel quite drowsy. It is just like being in
church.'

'"Lots of people act well,' answered the Miller; 'but very few people talk well, which shows
that talking is much the more difficult thing of
the two, and much the finer thing also'; and he
looked sternly across the table at his little son,
who felt so ashamed of himself that he hung his
head down, and grew quite scarlet, and began to
cry into his tea. However, he was so young that
you must excuse him."

"Is that the end of the story?" asked the Water-rat.
끝 이야기

"Certainly not," answered the Linnet, "that is the beginning."
물론 아니다, 당치도 않다 · 홍방울새 · 시작

"Then you are quite behind the age," said the Water-rat. "Every good story-teller nowadays starts with the end, and then goes on to the beginning, and concludes with the middle. That is the new method. I heard all about it the other day from a critic who was walking round the pond with a young man. He spoke of the matter at great length, and I am sure he must have been right, for he had blue spectacles and a bald head, and whenever the young man made any remark, he always answered 'Pooh!' But pray go on with your story. I like the Miller immensely. I have all kinds of beautiful sentiments myself, so there is a great sympathy between us."
아주, 꽤 · 시대에 뒤떨어진 · 이야기꾼 · 요즘에는, 오늘날에 · 시작하다 · 끝, 마지막 · 끝나다; 끝내다, 마치다 · 중앙, (한)가운데, 중간 · 방법, 체계성 · 일전에, 며칠 전에 · 비평가, 평론가 · 연못 · 말하다 · 장황하게, 지루하게; 상세하게 · 안경 · 대머리 · ~할 때마다 · 언급[말/논평/발언]하다 · = please · 엄청나게, 대단히 · 종류 · 정서, 감정 · 공감, 지지, 동의 · ~사이에

"Well," said the Linnet, hopping now on one
leg and now on the other, "as soon as the winter
was over, and the primroses began to open their
pale yellow stars, the Miller said to his wife that
he would go down and see little Hans.

"'Why, what a good heart you have!' cried his
Wife; 'you are always thinking of others. And
mind you take the big basket with you for the
flowers.'

"So the Miller tied the sails of the windmill
together with a strong iron chain, and went
down the hill with the basket on his arm.

"'Good morning, little Hans,' said the Miller.

"'Good morning,' said Hans, leaning on his
spade, and smiling from ear to ear.

"'And how have you been all the winter?'
said the Miller.

"'Well, really,' cried Hans, 'it is very good of
you to ask, very good indeed. I am afraid I had
rather a hard time of it, but now the spring has
come, and I am quite happy, and all my flowers

77

are doing well.'

"'We often talked of you during the winter, [자주, 종종] [~동안] Hans,' said the Miller, 'and wondered how you [궁금해 하다] were getting on.' [지내다, 꾸려 나가다]

"'That was kind of you,' said Hans; 'I was [친절한] half afraid you had forgotten me.' [염려하는] [잊어버리다]

"'Hans, I am surprised at you,' said the Miller; 'friendship never forgets. That is the won- [~에 놀라다] [우정] derful thing about it, but I am afraid you don't understand the poetry of life. How lovely your [시(= verse); 우아함] primroses are looking, by-the-bye"! [그런데, 말이 났으니 말이지(by the way)]

"'They are certainly very lovely,' said Hans, [틀림없이, 분명히] 'and it is a most lucky thing for me that I have so [운이 좋은, 행운의] many. I am going to bring them into the market [~하려고 하다] [시장] and sell them to the Burgomaster's daughter, [팔다] [(네덜란드의) 시장(市長)] [딸] and buy back my wheelbarrow with the money.' [도로 사오다] [외바퀴 손수레]

"'Buy back your wheelbarrow? You don't mean to say you have sold it? What a very stu- [뜻하다, 의미하다] [팔다] [어리석은 (=foolish, silly)] pid thing to do!'

"'Well, the fact is,' said Hans, 'that I was [사실, 실제] obliged to. You see the winter was a very bad [하는 수 없이 …하다] [알다] [겨울] [곤경]

78

time for me, and I really had no money at all to buy bread with. So I first sold the silver buttons off my Sunday coat, and then I sold my silver chain, and then I sold my big pipe, and at last I sold my wheelbarrow. But I am going to buy them all back again now.'

"'Hans,' said the Miller, 'I will give you my wheelbarrow. It is not in very good repair; indeed, one side is gone, and there is something wrong with the wheel-spokes; but in spite of that I will give it to you. I know it is very generous of me, and a great many people would think me extremely foolish for parting with it, but I am not like the rest of the world. I think that generosity is the essence of friendship, and, besides, I have got a new wheelbarrow for myself. Yes, you may set your mind at ease, I will give you my wheelbarrow.'

"'Well, really, that is generous of you,' said little Hans, and his funny round face glowed all over with pleasure.

'I can easily put it in repair, as I have a plank
쉽게   수리, 보수   널빤지, 판자
of wood in the house.'
나무

"'A plank of wood'! said the Miller; 'why,

that is just what I want for the roof of my barn.
지붕   곳간, 헛간
There is a very large hole in it, and the corn will
큰   구멍   옥수수
all get damp if I don't stop it up. How lucky you
축축한, 눅눅한
mentioned it! It is quite remarkable how one
말하다, 언급[거론]하다   놀랄 만한, 놀라운, 주목할 만한
good action always breeds another. I have given
행동, 행위   낳다, 야기하다, ~을 불러오다
you my wheelbarrow, and now you are going

to give me your plank. Of course, the wheelbar-

row is worth far more than the plank, but true,
가치 있는
friendship never notices things like that. Pray
주목하다
get it at once, and I will set to work at my barn
당장, 즉시   일을 시작하다
this very day.'
바로 오늘

"'Certainly,' cried little Hans, and he ran into

the shed and dragged the plank out.
(작은) 헛간   (힘들여) 끌다
"'It is not a very big plank,' said the Miller,

looking at it, 'and I am afraid that after I have
처다보다   ~뒤에
mended my barn-roof there won't be any left
수리하다, 고치다
for you to mend the wheelbarrow with; but, of

course, that is not my fault. And now, as I have
잘못, 실수

80

given you my wheelbarrow, I am sure you would
like to give me some flowers in return. Here is
the basket, and mind you fill it quite full.'

"'Quite full?' said little Hans, rather sorrow-
fully, for it was really a very big basket, and he
knew that if he filled it he would have no flowers
left for the market and he was very anxious to
get his silver buttons back.

"'Well, really,' answered the Miller, 'as I have
given you my wheelbarrow, I don't think that it
is much to ask you for a few flowers. I may be
wrong, but I should have thought that friendship, true friendship, was quite free from selfishness of any kind.'

"'My dear friend, my best friend,' cried little
Hans, 'you are welcome to all the flowers in my
garden. I would much sooner have your good
opinion than my silver buttons, any day.'; and
he ran and plucked all his pretty primroses, and
filled the Miller's basket.

"'Good-bye, little Hans,' said the Miller, as he

went up the hill with the plank on his shoulder,
언덕 / 널빤지, 판자 / 어깨

and the big basket in his hand.

"'Good-bye,' said little Hans, and he began to

dig away quite merrily, he was so pleased about
계속해서 파다 / 즐겁게, 유쾌하게 / 쾌적한, 즐거운, 기분 좋은

the wheelbarrow.

"The next day he was nailing up some hon-
못질하다, 못을 박다 / 인동(덩굴식물의 일종)

eysuckle against the porch, when he heard the
현관

Miller's voice calling to him from the road. So
도로, 길

he jumped off the ladder, and ran down the gar-
뛰어 내리다 / 사다리

den, and looked over the wall.

"There was the Miller with a large sack of
부대, 자루

flour on his back.
밀가루 / 등

"'Dear little Hans,' said the Miller, 'would

you mind carrying this sack of flour for me to
운반하다, 나르다

market?'
시장

"'Oh, I am so sorry,' said Hans, 'but I am re-

ally very busy to-day. I have got all my creepers
바쁜 / 덩굴 식물

to nail up, and all my flowers to water, and all
못을 박아 걸다 / 물을 주다

my grass to roll.'
잔디

"'Well, really,' said the Miller, 'I think that,

considering that I am going to give you my
…을 고려[감안]하면

wheelbarrow, it is rather unfriendly of you to re-
비우호적인, 불친절한, 쌀쌀맞은   거절하다
fuse.'

"'Oh, don't say that,' cried little Hans, 'I
wouldn't be unfriendly for the whole world'; and
전체[전부]의, 모든, 온전한
he ran in for his cap, and trudged off with the
모자   (무거운 것을 들고) 느릿느릿 걷다
big sack on his shoulders.
커다란 자루[부대]

"It was a very hot day, and the road was ter-
더운, 뜨거운   도로, 길
ribly dusty, and before Hans had reached the
먼지투성이의   도착하다
sixth milestone he was so tired that he had to
(돌로 된) 마일표   지친, 피곤한   ~해야 하다
sit down and rest. However, he went on bravely,
쉬다, 휴식하다   용감하게
and as last he reached the market.
마침내, 결국

"After he had waited there some time, he
기다리다
sold the sack of flour for a very good price,
팔다   밀가루 한 자루   값, 가격
and then he returned home at once, for he was
돌아오다   곧, 즉시, 당장
afraid that if he stopped too late he might meet
~을 두려워하다   늦은, 지연된   만나다
some robbers on the way.
강도   도중에, 가는 길에

"'It has certainly been a hard day,' said little
분명히, 틀림없이   힘든, 고단한
Hans to himself as he was going to bed, 'but I
am glad I did not refuse the Miller, for he is my
기쁜, 고마운   거절하다
best friend, and, besides, he is going to give me
게다가
his wheelbarrow.'
외바퀴 수레

"Early the next morning the Miller came
down to get the money for his sack of flour, but
little Hans was so tired that he was still in bed.

"'Upon my word,' said the Miller, 'you are
very lazy. Really, considering that I am going
to give you my wheelbarrow, I think you might
work harder. Idleness is a great sin, and I certainly don't like any of my friends to be idle or
sluggish. You must not mind my speaking quite
plainly to you. Of course I should not dream of
doing so if I were not your friend. But what is
the good of friendship if one cannot say exactly
what one means? Anybody can say charming
things and try to please and to flatter, but a true
friend always says unpleasant things, and does
not mind giving pain. Indeed, if he is a really
true friend he prefers it, for he knows that then
he is doing good.'

"'I am very sorry,' said little Hans, rubbing
his eyes and pulling off his night-cap, 'but I was
so tired that I thought I would lie in bed for a lit-

84

tle time, and listen to the birds singing. Do you know that I always work better after hearing the birds sing?'

"'Well, I am glad of that,' said the Miller, clapping little Hans on the back, 'for I want you to come up to the mill as soon as you are dressed, and mend my barn-roof for me.'

"Poor little Hans was very anxious to go and work in his garden, for his flowers had not been watered for two days, but he did not like to re-fuse the Miller, as he was such a good friend to him.

"'Do you think it would be unfriendly of me if I said I was busy?' he inquired in a shy and timid voice.

"'Well, really,' answered the Miller, 'I do not think it is much to ask of you, considering that I am going to give you my wheelbarrow; but of course if you refuse I will go and do it myself.'

"'Oh! on no account,' cried little Hans and he jumped out of bed, and dressed himself, and went up to the barn. He worked there all day long, till sunset, and at sunset the Miller came to see how he was getting on.

"'Have you mended the hole in the roof yet, little Hans?' cried the Miller in a cheery voice.

"'It is quite mended,' answered little Hans, coming down the ladder.

"'Ah!' said the Miller, 'there is no work so delightful as the work one does for others.'

"'It is certainly a great privilege to hear you talk,' answered little Hans, sitting down, and wiping his forehead, 'a very great privilege. But I am afraid I shall never have such beautiful ideas as you have.'

"'Oh! they will come to you,' said the Miller, 'but you must take more pains. At present you have only the practice of friendship; some day you will have the theory also.'

"'Do you really think I shall?' asked little Hans.

"'I have no doubt of it,' answered the Miller,

'but now that you have mended the roof, you had better go home and rest, for I want you to drive my sheep to the mountain to-morrow.'

"Poor little Hans was afraid to say anything to this, and early the next morning the Miller brought his sheep round to the cottage, and Hans started off with them to the mountain. It took him the whole day to get there and back; and when he returned he was so tired that he went off to sleep in his chair, and did not wake up till it was broad daylight.

"'What a delightful time I shall have in my garden,' he said, and he went to work at once.

"But somehow he was never able to look after his flowers at all, for his friend the Miller was always coming round and sending him off on long errands, or getting him to help at the mill. Little Hans was very much distressed at times, as he was afraid his flowers would think he had forgotten them, but he consoled himself by the reflection that the Miller was his best friend.

'Besides,' he used to say, 'he is going to give me
his wheelbarrow, and that is an act of pure generosity.'

"So little Hans worked away for the Miller, and the Miller said all kinds of beautiful things about friendship, which Hans took down in a note-book, and used to read over at night, for he was a very good scholar.

"Now it happened that one evening little Hans was sitting by his fireside when a loud rap came at the door. It was a very wild night, and the wind was blowing and roaring round the house so terribly that at first he thought it was merely the storm. But a second rap came, and then a third, louder than any of the others.

"'It is some poor traveller,' said little Hans to himself, and he ran to the door.

"There stood the Miller with a lantern in one hand and a big stick in the other.

"'Dear little Hans,' cried the Miller, 'I am in great trouble. My little boy has fallen off a lad-

게다가, 더욱이 · 순수한 너그러움 · 계속 일하다, 열심히 노력하다 · 온갖 종류의, 모든 종류의 · 쓰다, 기록하다 · 공책 · 읽다 · 학자, 모범생 · (~ 일이) 있다[발생하다/벌어지다] · 저녁 · 난롯가 · 세게 두드리는 소리 · 거친, 사나운 · 바람 · 불다 · 포효하다 · 끔찍하게, 무시무시하게 · 그저, 단순히 · 태풍, 폭풍 · 더욱 (소리가) 큰, 시끄러운 · 여행자 · 랜턴, 손전등 · 지팡이 · 곤경, 문제, 애 · 떨어지다

88

der and hurt himself, and I am going for the
Doctor. But he lives so far away, and it is such a
bad night, that it has just occurred to me that it
would be much better if you went instead of me.
You know I am going to give you my wheelbarrow, and so, it is only fair that you should do
something for me in return.'

"'Certainly,' cried little Hans, 'I take it quite
as a compliment your coming to me, and I will
start off at once. But you must lend me your
lantern, as the night is so dark that I am afraid I
might fall into the ditch.'

"'I am very sorry,' answered the Miller, 'but
it is my new lantern, and it would be a great loss
to me if anything happened to it.'

"'Well, never mind, I will do without it,' cried
little Hans, and he took down his great fur coat,
and his warm scarlet cap, and tied a muffler
round his throat, and started off.

"What a dreadful storm it was! The night
was so black that little Hans could hardly see,

89

and the wind was so strong that he could scarce-
ly stand. However, he was very courageous, and
after he had been walking about three hours, he
arrived at the Doctor's house, and knocked at
the door.

"'Who is there?' cried the Doctor, putting his
head out of his bedroom window.

"'Little Hans, Doctor.'

"'What do you want, little Hans?'

"'The Miller's son has fallen from a ladder,
and has hurt himself, and the Miller wants you
to come at once.'

"'All right!' said the Doctor; and he ordered
his horse, and his big boots, and his lantern, and
came downstairs, and rode off in the direction of
the Miller's house, little Hans trudging behind
him.

"But the storm grew worse and worse, and
the rain fell in torrents, and little Hans could
not see where he was going, or keep up with the
horse.

At last he lost his way, and wandered off on
the moor, which was a very dangerous place,
as it was full of deep holes, and there poor little
Hans was drowned. His body was found the
next day by some goatherds, floating in a great
pool of water, and was brought back by them to
the cottage.

"Everybody went to little Hans' funeral, as
he was so popular, and the Miller was the chief
mourner.

"'As I was his best friend,' said the Miller, 'it
is only fair that I should have the best place'; so
he walked at the head of the procession in a long
black cloak, and every now and then he wiped
his eyes with a big pocket-handkerchief.

"'Little Hans is certainly a great loss to every
one,' said the Blacksmith, when the funeral was
over, and they were all seated comfortably in
the inn, drinking spiced wine and eating sweet
cakes.

"'A great loss to me at any rate,' answered
the Miller; 'why, I had as good as given him my
wheelbarrow, and now I really don't know what
to do with it. It is very much in my way at home,
and it is in such bad repair that I could not get
anything for it if I sold it. I will certainly take
care not to give away anything again. One always suffers for being generous.'"

"Well?" said the Water-rat, after a long
pause.

"Well, that is the end," said the Linnet.

"But what became of the Miller?" asked the
Water-rat.

"Oh! I really don't know," replied the Linnet;
"and I am sure that I don't care."

"It is quite evident then that you have no
sympathy in your nature," said the Water-rat.

"I am afraid you don't quite see the moral of
the story," remarked the Linnet.

"The what?" screamed the Water-rat.

"The moral."

"Do you mean to say that the story has a moral?"

"Certainly," said the Linnet.

"Well, really," said the Water-rat, in a very angry manner, "I think you should have told me that before you began. If you had done so, I certainly would not have listened to you; in fact, I should have said 'Pooh,' like the critic. However, I can say it now"; so he shouted out "Pooh" at the top of his voice, gave a whisk with his tail, and went back into his hole.

"And how do you like the Water-rat?" asked the Duck, who came paddling up some minutes afterwards. "He has a great many good points, but for my own part I have a mother's feelings, and I can never look at a confirmed bachelor without the tears coming into my eyes."

"I am rather afraid that I have annoyed him," answered the Linnet. "The fact is, that I told him a story with a moral."

"Ah! that is always a very dangerous thing to
do," said the Duck.

늘, 언제나   위험한, 험난한

And I quite agree with her.

~에 동의하다

비범한 로켓

The Remarkable Rocket

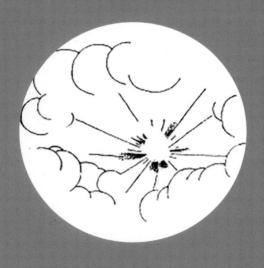

The King's son was going to be married, so there were general rejoicings. He had waited a whole year for his bride, and at last she had arrived.

She was a Russian Princess, and had driven all the way from Finland in a sledge drawn by six reindeer. The sledge was shaped like a great golden swan, and between the swan's wings lay the little Princess herself.

Her long ermine-cloak reached right down to her feet, on her head was a tiny cap of silver tissue, and she was as pale as the Snow Palace in which she had always lived.

So pale was she that as she drove through the streets all the people wondered.

"She is like a white rose!" they cried, and they threw down flowers on her from the balconies.

At the gate of the Castle the Prince was waiting to receive her. He had dreamy violet eyes, and his hair was like fine gold. When he saw her he sank upon one knee, and kissed her hand.

"Your picture was beautiful," he murmured, "but you are more beautiful than your picture"; and the little Princess blushed.

"She was like a white rose before," said a young Page to his neighbour, "but she is like a red rose now"; and the whole Court was delighted.

For the next three days everybody went about saying, "White rose, Red rose, Red rose, White rose"; and the King gave orders that the Page's salary was to be doubled. As he received no salary at all this was not of much use to him,

but it was considered a great honour, and was
duly published in the Court Gazette.

When the three days were over the marriage
was celebrated. It was a magnificent ceremony,
and the bride and bridegroom walked hand in
hand under a canopy of purple velvet embroidered with little pearls.

Then there was a State Banquet, which lasted for five hours. The Prince and Princess sat
at the top of the Great Hall and drank out of a
cup of clear crystal. Only true lovers could drink
out of this cup, for if false lips touched it, it grew
grey and dull and cloudy.

"It's quite clear that they love each other,"
said the little Page, "as clear as crystal!" and the
King doubled his salary a second time. "What an
honour!" cried all the courtiers.

After the banquet there was to be a Ball. The
bride and bridegroom were to dance the Rose-
dance together, and the King had promised to
play the flute.

He played very badly, but no one had ever
dared to tell him so, because he was the King.
Indeed, he knew only two airs, and was never
quite certain which one he was playing; but it
made no matter, for, whatever he did, everybody cried out, "Charming! charming!"

The last item on the programme was a grand
display of fireworks, to be let off exactly at midnight. The little Princess had never seen a fire-
work in her life, so the King had given orders
that the Royal Pyrotechnist should be in atten-
dance on the day of her marriage.

"What are fireworks like?" she had asked the
Prince, one morning, as she was walking on the
terrace.

"They are like the Aurora Borealis," said the
King, who always answered questions that were
addressed to other people, "only much more
natural. I prefer them to stars myself, as you always know when they are going to appear, and
they are as delightful as my own flute-playing.

You must certainly see them."

So at the end of the King's garden a great stand had been set up, and as soon as the Royal Pyrotechnist had put everything in its proper place, the fireworks began to talk to each other.

"The world is certainly very beautiful," cried a little Squib. "Just look at those yellow tulips. Why! if they were real crackers they could not be lovelier. I am very glad I have travelled. Travel improves the mind wonderfully, and does away with all one's prejudices."

"The King's garden is not the world, you foolish squib," said a big Roman Candle; "the world is an enormous place, and it would take you three days to see it thoroughly."

"Any place you love is the world to you," exclaimed a pensive Catherine Wheel, who had been attached to an old deal box in early life, and prided herself on her broken heart; "but love is not fashionable any more, the poets have killed it. They wrote so much about it that no-

101

body believed them, and I am not surprised.
믿다   놀라지 않는다

True love suffers, and is silent. I remember my-
진실한   시달리다, 고통받다   침묵을 지키는, 조용한

self once--But it is no matter now. Romance is a
연애, 로맨스

thing of the past."
과거, 지난날

"Nonsense!" said the Roman Candle, "Ro-
터무니없는[말도 안 되는] 생각[말], 허튼소리

mance never dies. It is like the moon, and lives
죽다   달

for ever. The bride and bridegroom, for in-
영원히   예를 들어

stance, love each other very dearly. I heard all
끔찍이, 깊이, 소중하게

about them this morning from a brown-paper
갈색 종이

cartridge, who happened to be staying in the
탄약통

same drawer as myself, and knew the latest
서랍   최근의

Court news."

But the Catherine Wheel shook her head.
고개를 흔들다

"Romance is dead, Romance is dead, Romance

is dead," she murmured. She was one of those
중얼거리다

people who think that, if you say the same thing

over and over a great many times, it becomes
여러 번 되풀이하여[거듭거듭]

true in the end.

Suddenly, a sharp, dry cough was heard, and
갑자기, 별안간   날카로운   건조한 (헛)기침

they all looked round.

It came from a tall, supercilious-looking
키 큰   거만해 보이는, 오만하게 생긴
Rocket, who was tied to the end of a long stick.
         묶다, 매다   긴   막대기
He always coughed before he made any obser-
늘, 항상 (헛)기침 하다 ~전에   논평, 의견
vation, so as to attract attention.
          눈길을 끌다, 주의를 끌다, 관심을 끌다

"Ahem! ahem!" he said, and everybody lis-

tened except the poor Catherine Wheel, who
      ~만 빼고, ~을 제외하고
was still shaking her head, and murmuring,
     아직도, 여전히
"Romance is dead."

"Order! order!" cried out a Cracker. He was
질서[규칙]를 지켜요!
something of a politician, and had always taken
            정치인, 정치가
a prominent part in the local elections, so he
중요한, 두드러진, 현저한   지방 선거.
knew the proper Parliamentary expressions to
        적절한, 제대로 된   의회의, 의회가 있는   표현
use.
사용하다

"Quite dead," whispered the Catherine
             속삭이다
Wheel, and she went off to sleep.
                자리를 뜨다

As soon as there was perfect silence, the
~하자마자   완벽한, 완전한 고요, 침묵
Rocket coughed a third time and began.

He spoke with a very slow, distinct voice,
말하다   느린   뚜렷한, 분명한
as if he was dictating his memoirs, and always
마치 ~처럼   받아쓰게 하다, 구술하다 회고록, 전기, 체험기
looked over the shoulder of the person to whom
                어깨   사람, 개인
he was talking.

103

In fact, he had a most distinguished manner.

"How fortunate it is for the King's son," he remarked, "that he is to be married on the very day on which I am to be let off. Really, if it had been arranged beforehand, it could not have turned out better for him; but, Princes are always lucky."

"Dear me!" said the little Squib, "I thought it was quite the other way, and that we were to be let off in the Prince's honour."

"It may be so with you," he answered; "indeed, I have no doubt that it is, but with me it is different. I am a very remarkable Rocket, and come of remarkable parents. My mother was the most celebrated Catherine Wheel of her day, and was renowned for her graceful dancing. When she made her great public appearance she spun round nineteen times before she went out, and each time that she did so she threw into the air seven pink stars. She was three feet and a half in diameter, and made of the very

best gunpowder. My father was a Rocket like
myself, and of French extraction. He flew so
high that the people were afraid that he would
never come down again. He did, though, for he
was of a kindly disposition, and he made a most
brilliant descent in a shower of golden rain. The
newspapers wrote about his performance in
very flattering terms. Indeed, the Court Gazette
called him a triumph of Pylotechnic art."

"Pyrotechnic, Pyrotechnic, you mean," said a
Bengal Light; "I know it is Pyrotechnic, for I saw
it written on my own canister."

"Well, I said Pylotechnic," answered the
Rocket, in a severe tone of voice, and the Bengal
Light felt so crushed that he began at once to
bully the little squibs, in order to show that he
was still a person of some importance.

"I was saying," continued the Rocket, "I was
saying--What was I saying?"

"You were talking about yourself," replied
the Roman Candle.

"Of course; I knew I was discussing some
논하다

interesting subject when I was so rudely inter-
흥미있는, 재미있는   주제, 문제, 사안   무례한, 예의 없는 방해하다

rupted. I hate rudeness and bad manners of
혐오하다, 싫어하다   태도, 예절

every kind, for I am extremely sensitive. No one
종류, 부류   극도로, 극심하게 예민한, 민감한

in the whole world is so sensitive as I am, I am
전체의, 전부의

quite sure of that."
꽤, 상당히, 아주

"What is a sensitive person?" said the Crack-
사람, 개인

er to the Roman Candle.

"A person who, because he has corns him-
티눈

self, always treads on other people's toes," an-
(발을) 디디다, 밟다   발가락

swered the Roman Candle in a low whisper; and
낮은 속삭임

the Cracker nearly exploded with laughter.
거의   웃음을 터뜨리다

"Pray, what are you laughing at?" inquired
~을 비웃다   따져 묻다

the Rocket; "I am not laughing."

"I am laughing because I am happy," replied

the Cracker.

"That is a very selfish reason," said the Rock-
이기적인   이유, 근거

et angrily. "What right have you to be happy?
성내며, 화가 나서   권리

You should be thinking about others. In fact,
~에 대해 생각하다   다른 사람들

you should be thinking about me. I am always

thinking about myself, and I expect everybody
기대하다, 바라다

else to do the same. That is what is called sympathy. It is a beautiful virtue, and I possess it in
a high degree. Suppose, for instance, anything
happened to me to-night, what a misfortune
that would be for every one! The Prince and
Princess would never be happy again, their
whole married life would be spoiled; and as for
the King, I know he would not get over it. Really, when I begin to reflect on the importance
of my position, I am almost moved to tears."

"If you want to give pleasure to others," cried
the Roman Candle, "you had better keep yourself dry."

"Certainly," exclaimed the Bengal Light, who
was now in better spirits; "that is only common
sense."

"Common sense, indeed!" said the Rocket
indignantly; "you forget that I am very uncom-
mon, and very remarkable. Why, anybody can
have common sense, provided that they have no
imagination. But I have imagination, for I never

107

think of things as they really are; I always think
사물을 있는 그대로 보다[생각하다]
of them as being quite different. As for keeping
꽤, 아주   다른, 차이가 나는
myself dry, there is evidently no one here who
분명히, 눈에 띄게 (=obviously)
can at all appreciate an emotional nature. For-
진가를 알아보다; 고마워하다   정서적인, 감정의   천성, 본성
tunately for myself, I don't care. The only thing
상관 없다
that sustains one through life is the conscious-
살아가게[존재하게/지탱하게] 하다   자각, 의식
ness of the immense inferiority of everybody
엄청난, 어마어마한   열등함
else, and this is a feeling that I have always cul-
기르다, 함양하다
tivated. But none of you have any hearts. Here
마음, 가슴
you are laughing and making merry just as if the
즐거운, 명랑한   마치 ~인 것처럼
Prince and Princess had not just been married."

"Well, really," exclaimed a small Fire-
소리치다   작은
balloon, "why not? It is a most joyful occasion,
가장   기쁜   행사, 의식, 축하
and when I soar up into the air I intend to tell
숫구치다, 날아오르다   ~할 작정이다[생각이다]
the stars all about it. You will see them twinkle
반짝반짝 빛나다
when I talk to them about the pretty bride."
예쁜, 귀여운, 사랑스러운
"Ah! what a trivial view of life!" said the
사소한, 하찮은
Rocket; "but it is only what I expected. There
기대하다
is nothing in you; you are hollow and empty.
(속이) 빈, 공허한   비어 있는, 공허한
Why, perhaps the Prince and Princess may go
아마도, 어쩌면
to live in a country where there is a deep river,
나라   깊은

and perhaps they may have one only son, a little

fair-haired boy with violet eyes like the Prince
머리카락이 옅은 색인, 금발의   보랏빛의

himself; and perhaps some day he may go out to
어느 날, 언젠가   산책하러 가다

walk with his nurse; and perhaps the nurse may
보모, 간호사

go to sleep under a great elder-tree; and perhaps
딱총나무

the little boy may fall into the deep river and be
~에 빠지다   강

drowned. What a terrible misfortune! Poor peo-
익사하다, 빠져 죽다   끔찍한, 가혹한   불운, 불행   불쌍한, 가엾은

ple, to lose their only son! It is really too dread-
잃다, 상실하다   끔찍한, 혹독한

ful! I shall never get over it."
극복하다, ~을 이겨내다

"But they have not lost their only son," said

the Roman Candle; "no misfortune has hap-
불행, 불운   일어나다, 발생하다

pened to them at all."

"I never said that they had," replied the
대답하다

Rocket; "I said that they might. If they had lost

their only son there would be no use in saying
~해도 소용없다

anything more about the matter. I hate people
무척 싫어하다

who cry over spilt milk. But when I think that
쏟다, 엎지르다

they might lose their only son, I certainly am

very much affected."
(강한 정서적) 충격을 주다, 깊은 슬픔[연민]을 유발하다

"You certainly are!" cried the Bengal Light.

"In fact, you are the most affected person I ever
악영향을 미치다

met."

"You are the rudest person I ever met," said
무례한, 예의 없는
the Rocket, "and you cannot understand my
이해하다, 알다
friendship for the Prince."
우정

"Why, you don't even know him," growled
으르렁거리다
the Roman Candle.

"I never said I knew him," answered the
Rocket. "I dare say that if I knew him I should
감히 ~하다
not be his friend at all. It is a very dangerous
위험한
thing to know one's friends."

"You had really better keep yourself dry,"
정말로   ~하는 게 더 낫다
said the Fire-balloon. "That is the important
중요한
thing."

"Very important for you, I have no doubt,"
중요한   의심, 의혹
answered the Rocket, "but I shall weep if I
울다, 눈물을 흘리다
choose"; and he actually burst into real tears,
고르다, 선택하다   실제로   눈물을 터뜨리다
which flowed down his stick like rain-drops, and
흘러내리다   막대기   빗방울
nearly drowned two little beetles, who were just
거의   익사하다, 물에 빠져 죽다   딱정벌레
thinking of setting up house together, and were
집을 짓다   함께
looking for a nice dry spot to live in.
~을 찾다   지점, 곳, 장소

"He must have a truly romantic nature," said
the Catherine Wheel, "for he weeps when there
is nothing at all to weep about"; and she heaved
a deep sigh, and thought about the deal box.

But the Roman Candle and the Bengal Light
were quite indignant, and kept saying, "Humbug! humbug!" at the top of their voices. They
were extremely practical, and whenever they
objected to anything they called it humbug.

Then the moon rose like a wonderful silver
shield; and the stars began to shine, and a sound
of music came from the palace.

The Prince and Princess were leading the
dance. They danced so beautifully that the
tall white lilies peeped in at the window and
watched them, and the great red poppies nodded their heads and beat time.

Then ten o'clock struck, and then eleven, and
then twelve, and at the last stroke of midnight
every one came out on the terrace, and the King
sent for the Royal Pyrotechnist.

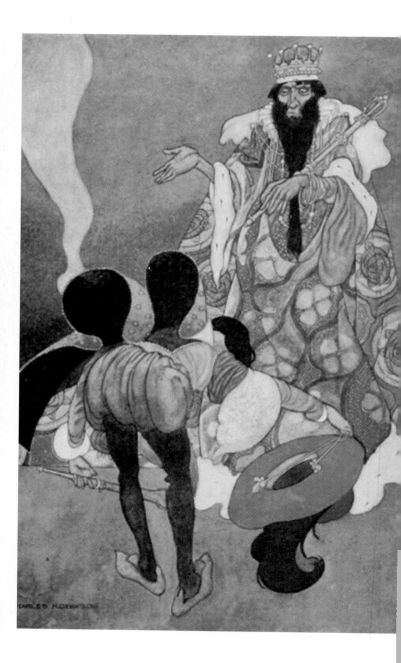

"Let the fireworks begin," said the King; and the Royal Pyrotechnist made a low bow, and marched down to the end of the garden. He had six attendants with him, each of whom carried a lighted torch at the end of a long pole.

It was certainly a magnificent display.

Whizz! Whizz! went the Catherine Wheel, as she spun round and round. Boom! Boom! went the Roman Candle. Then the Squibs danced all over the place, and the Bengal Lights made everything look scarlet.

"Good-bye," cried the Fire-balloon, as he soared away, dropping tiny blue sparks. Bang! Bang! answered the Crackers, who were enjoying themselves immensely.

Every one was a great success except the Remarkable Rocket. He was so damp with crying that he could not go off at all. The best thing in him was the gunpowder, and that was so wet with tears that it was of no use. All his poor relations, to whom he would never speak, except

with a sneer, shot up into the sky like wonder-
냉소(冷笑)하여, 비웃으며

ful golden flowers with blossoms of fire. Huzza!
황금 꽃   불의 꽃

Huzza! cried the Court; and the little Princess
대궐, 궁궐, 궁전

laughed with pleasure.

"I suppose they are reserving me for some
짐작하다, 추측하다   따로 잡아[남겨] 두다

grand occasion," said the Rocket; "no doubt that
(특정한) 때, 행사, 의식

is what it means," and he looked more supercil-
거만한, 남을 얕보는

ious than ever.

The next day the workmen came to put ev-
다음 날   노동[노무]자, 일군

erything tidy.
정돈하다, 정리하다

"This is evidently a deputation," said the
분명히   대표[사절]단

Rocket; "I will receive them with becoming dig-
환영[접대]하다   위엄, 품위

nity" so he put his nose in the air, and began

to frown severely as if he were thinking about
얼굴[눈살]을 찌푸리다[찡그리다]

some very important subject.
중요한   주제

But they took no notice of him at all till they
…을 무시하다, ~을 알아차리지 못하다

were just going away. Then one of them caught
…을 찾아내다, 언뜻 보다

sight of him.

"Hallo!" he cried, "what a bad rocket!" and

he threw him over the wall into the ditch.
던지다   ~위로   벽, 담   도랑, 배수로

114

"BAD Rocket? BAD Rocket?" he said, as he whirled through the air; "impossible! GRAND Rocket, that is what the man said. BAD and GRAND sound very much the same, indeed they often are the same"; and he fell into the mud.

"It is not comfortable here," he remarked, "but no doubt it is some fashionable watering-place, and they have sent me away to recruit my health. My nerves are certainly very much shattered, and I require rest."

Then a little Frog, with bright jewelled eyes, and a green mottled coat, swam up to him.

"A new arrival, I see!" said the Frog. "Well, after all there is nothing like mud. Give me rainy weather and a ditch, and I am quite happy. Do you think it will be a wet afternoon? I am sure I hope so, but the sky is quite blue and cloudless. What a pity!"

"Ahem! ahem!" said the Rocket, and he began to cough.

"What a delightful voice you have!" cried the
Frog. "Really it is quite like a croak, and croak-
ing is of course the most musical sound in the
world. You will hear our glee-club this evening.
We sit in the old duck pond close by the farmer's
house, and as soon as the moon rises we begin.
It is so entrancing that everybody lies awake to
listen to us. In fact, it was only yesterday that I
heard the farmer's wife say to her mother that
she could not get a wink of sleep at night on account of us. It is most gratifying to find oneself
so popular."

"Ahem! ahem!" said the Rocket angrily. He
was very much annoyed that he could not get a
word in.

"A delightful voice, certainly," continued the
Frog; "I hope you will come over to the duck-
pond. I am off to look for my daughters. I have
six beautiful daughters, and I am so afraid the
Pike may meet them. He is a perfect monster,
and would have no hesitation in breakfasting off

them. Well, good-bye: I have enjoyed our conversation very much, I assure you."

"Conversation, indeed!" said the Rocket. "You have talked the whole time yourself. That is not conversation."

"Somebody must listen," answered the Frog, "and I like to do all the talking myself. It saves time, and prevents arguments."

"But I like arguments," said the Rocket.

"I hope not," said the Frog complacently. "Arguments are extremely vulgar, for everybody in good society holds exactly the same opinions. Good-bye a second time; I see my daughters in the distance." and the little Frog swam away.

"You are a very irritating person," said the Rocket, "and very ill-bred. I hate people who talk about themselves, as you do, when one wants to talk about oneself, as I do. It is what I call selfishness, and selfishness is a most detestable thing, especially to any one of my temperament, for I am well known for my sympathetic nature. In fact, you should take example by me; you could not possibly have a better model. Now that you have the chance you had better avail yourself of it, for I am going back to Court almost immediately. I am a great favourite at Court; in fact, the Prince and Princess were married yesterday in my honour. Of course you know nothing of these matters, for you are a provincial."

"There is no good talking to him," said a Dragon-fly, who was sitting on the top of a large brown bulrush; "no good at all, for he has gone away."

"Well, that is his loss, not mine," answered the Rocket. "I am not going to stop talking to him merely because he pays no attention. I like hearing myself talk. It is one of my greatest pleasures. I often have long conversations all by myself, and I am so clever that sometimes I don't understand a single word of what I am saying."

"Then you should certainly lecture on Philosophy," said the Dragon- fly; and he spread a pair of lovely gauze wings and soared away into the sky.

"How very silly of him not to stay here!" said the Rocket. "I am sure that he has not often got such a chance of improving his mind. However, I don't care a bit. Genius like mine is sure to be appreciated some day"; and he sank down a little deeper into the mud.

After some time a large White Duck swam up to him. She had yellow legs, and webbed feet, and was considered a great beauty on account of her waddle.

"Quack, quack, quack," she said. "What a curious shape you are! May I ask were you born like that, or is it the result of an accident?"

"It is quite evident that you have always lived in the country," answered the Rocket, "otherwise you would know who I am. However, I excuse your ignorance. It would be unfair to

expect other people to be as remarkable as oneself. You will no doubt be surprised to hear that
I can fly up into the sky, and come down in a
shower of golden rain."

"I don't think much of that," said the Duck,

"as I cannot see what use it is to any one. Now, if
you could plough the fields like the ox, or draw
a cart like the horse, or look after the sheep like
the collie-dog, that would be something."

"My good creature," cried the Rocket in a
very haughty tone of voice, "I see that you be-
long to the lower orders. A person of my position is never useful. We have certain accom-
plishments, and that is more than sufficient. I
have no sympathy myself with industry of any
kind, least of all with such industries as you
seem to recommend. Indeed, I have always been
of opinion that hard work is simply the refuge of
people who have nothing whatever to do."

"Well, well," said the Duck, who was of a

very peaceable disposition, and never quarrelled

with any one, "everybody has different tastes. I
hope, at any rate, that you are going to take up
your residence here."

"Oh! dear no," cried the Rocket. "I am
merely a visitor, a distinguished visitor. The fact
is that I find this place rather tedious. There is
neither society here, nor solitude. In fact, it is
essentially suburban. I shall probably go back to
Court, for I know that I am destined to make a
sensation in the world."

"I had thoughts of entering public life once
myself," remarked the Duck; "there are so many
things that need reforming. Indeed, I took
the chair at a meeting some time ago, and we
passed resolutions condemning everything that
we did not like. However, they did not seem to
have much effect. Now I go in for domesticity,
and look after my family."

"I am made for public life," said the Rocket,
"and so are all my relations, even the humblest
of them. Whenever we appear we excite great

121

attention. I have not actually appeared myself,
주의 (집중),주목, 관심, 흥미   나타나다
but when I do so it will be a magnificent sight.
                                                    장관
As for domesticity, it ages one rapidly, and
                                              빨리, 급속히, 신속히
distracts one's mind from higher things."
(정신이) 집중이 안 되게[산만하게/산란하게] 하다

"Ah! the higher things of life, how fine they
              더 중요한, 더 높은
are!" said the Duck; "and that reminds me how
                                        상기시키다, 기억나게 하다
hungry I feel": and she swam away down the
배고픈, 굶주린
stream, saying, "Quack, quack, quack."
개울, 시내

"Come back! come back!" screamed the
                                              비명을 지르다
Rocket, "I have a great deal to say to you"; but
                  할 말이 아주 많은
the Duck paid no attention to him.
              관심을 주지 않다, 주목하지 않다

"I am glad that she has gone," he said to
              기쁜, 즐거운, 고마운
himself, "she has a decidedly middle-class
                            확실히, 분명히   중산층의
mind"; and he sank a little deeper still into the
                            가라앉다
mud, and began to think about the loneliness of
                                              고독, 외로움
genius, when suddenly two little boys in white
천재   갑자기
smocks came running down the bank, with a
(옷이 더러워지지 않도록 위에 걸치는) 작업복[덧옷]   둑, 제방
kettle and some faggots.
주전자   (땔감용) 나무 한 단

"This must be the deputation," said the
                            대표[사절]단
Rocket, and he tried to look very dignified.
              시도하다, 애쓰다   위엄[품위] 있는

"Hallo!" cried one of the boys, "look at this
이봐, 야   소리치다
old stick! I wonder how it came here"; and he
막대기   궁금해 하다, 이상해 하다
picked the rocket out of the ditch.
집다   도랑

"OLD Stick!" said the Rocket, "impossible!

GOLD Stick, that is what he said. Gold Stick is

very complimentary. In fact, he mistakes me for
칭찬하는   오해[오인]하다, 잘못 판단하다
one of the Court dignitaries!"
고위 관리 (= VIP)

"Let us put it into the fire!" said the other

boy, "it will help to boil the kettle."
끓다, 끓이다

So they piled the faggots together, and put
(차곡차곡) 쌓다[포개다]
the Rocket on top, and lit the fire.
불을 붙이다[켜다](light의 과거, 과거분사)

"This is magnificent," cried the Rocket, "they
참으로 아름다운[감명 깊은/훌륭한]
are going to let me off in broad day-light, so that
백주 대낮에
every one can see me."

"We will go to sleep now," they said, "and

when we wake up the kettle will be boiled"; and
잠을 깨다   주전자   끓다
they lay down on the grass, and shut their eyes.
다   잔디, 풀   눈을 감다

The Rocket was very damp, so he took a long
축축한, 눅눅한
time to burn. At last, however, the fire caught
불타다   마침내, 결국   하지만, 어쨌든
him.

"Now I am going off!" he cried, and he made himself very stiff and straight. "I know I shall go much higher than the stars, much higher than the moon, much higher than the sun. In fact, I shall go so high that--"

Fizz! Fizz! Fizz! and he went straight up into the air.

"Delightful!" he cried, "I shall go on like this for ever. What a success I am!"

But nobody saw him.

Then he began to feel a curious tingling sensation all over him.

"Now I am going to explode," he cried. "I shall set the whole world on fire, and make such a noise that nobody will talk about anything else for a whole year."

And he certainly did explode. Bang! Bang! Bang! went the gunpowder. There was no doubt about it.

But nobody heard him, not even the two little boys, for they were sound asleep.

124

Then all that was left of him was the stick,
and this fell down on the back of a Goose who
was taking a walk by the side of the ditch.

"Good heavens!" cried the Goose. "It is going
to rain sticks"; and she rushed into the water.

"I knew I should create a great sensation,"
gasped the Rocket, and he went out.

캔터빌의 유령

The Canterville Ghost

1

When Mr. Hiram B. Otis, the American
Minister, bought Canterville Chase,
every one told him he was doing a very foolish
thing, as there was no doubt at all that the place
was haunted. Indeed, Lord Canterville himself,
who was a man of the most punctilious honour,
had felt it his duty to mention the fact to Mr.
Otis when they came to discuss terms.

"We have not cared to live in the place
ourselves," said Lord Canterville, "since my
grandaunt, the Dowager Duchess of Bolton, was
frightened into a fit, from which she never really

recovered, by two skeleton hands being placed on her shoulders as she was dressing for dinner, and I feel bound to tell you, Mr. Otis, that the ghost has been seen by several living members of my family, as well as by the rector of the parish, the Rev. Augustus Dampier, who is a Fellow of King's College, Cambridge. After the unfortunate accident to the Duchess, none of our younger servants would stay with us, and Lady Canterville often got very little sleep at night, in consequence of the mysterious noises that came from the corridor and the library."

"My Lord," answered the Minister, "I will take the furniture and the ghost at a valuation. I have come from a modern country, where we have everything that money can buy; and with all our spry young fellows painting the Old World red, and carrying off your best actors and prima-donnas, I reckon that if there were such a thing as a ghost in Europe, we'd have it at home in a very short time in one of our public muse-

ums, or on the road as a show."

"I fear that the ghost exists," said Lord Canterville, smiling, "though it may have resisted
the overtures of your enterprising impresarios.
It has been well known for three centuries, since
1584 in fact, and always makes its appearance
before the death of any member of our family."

"Well, so does the family doctor for that matter, Lord Canterville. But there is no such thing,
sir, as a ghost, and I guess the laws of Nature
are not going to be suspended for the British
aristocracy."

"You are certainly very natural in America,"
answered Lord Canterville, who did not quite
understand Mr. Otis's last observation, "and
if you don't mind a ghost in the house, it is all
right. Only you must remember I warned you."

A few weeks after this, the purchase was
concluded, and at the close of the season the
Minister and his family went down to Canterville Chase.

Mrs. Otis, who, as Miss Lucretia R. Tappan, of West 53d Street, had been a celebrated New York belle, was now a very handsome, middle-aged woman, with fine eyes, and a superb profile.

Many American ladies on leaving their native land adopt an appearance of chronic ill-health, under the impression that it is a form of European refinement, but Mrs. Otis had never fallen into this error.

She had a magnificent constitution, and a really wonderful amount of animal spirits. Indeed, in many respects, she was quite English, and was an excellent example of the fact that we have really everything in common with America nowadays, except, of course, language.

Her eldest son, christened Washington by his parents in a moment of patriotism, which he never ceased to regret, was a fair-haired, rather good-looking young man, who had qualified himself for American diplomacy by leading the

German at the Newport Casino for three suc-
cessive seasons, and even in London was well
known as an excellent dancer. Gardenias and
the peerage were his only weaknesses. Otherwise he was extremely sensible.

Miss Virginia E. Otis was a little girl of fif-
teen, lithe and lovely as a fawn, and with a fine
freedom in her large blue eyes.

She was a wonderful Amazon, and had once
raced old Lord Bilton on her pony twice round
the park, winning by a length and a half, just in
front of the Achilles statue, to the huge delight
of the young Duke of Cheshire, who proposed
for her on the spot, and was sent back to Eton
that very night by his guardians, in floods of
tears.

After Virginia came the twins, who were
usually called "The Star and Stripes," as they
were always getting swished. They were delightful boys, and, with the exception of the worthy
Minister, the only true republicans of the family.

As Canterville Chase is seven miles from Ascot, the nearest railway station, Mr. Otis had telegraphed for a waggonette to meet them, and they started on their drive in high spirits. It was a lovely July evening, and the air was delicate with the scent of the pinewoods. Now and then they heard a wood-pigeon brooding over its own sweet voice, or saw, deep in the rustling fern, the burnished breast of the pheasant. Little squirrels peered at them from the beech-trees as they went by, and the rabbits scudded away through the brushwood and over the mossy knolls, with their white tails in the air.

As they entered the avenue of Canterville Chase, however, the sky became suddenly over-cast with clouds, a curious stillness seemed to hold the atmosphere, a great flight of rooks passed silently over their heads, and, before they reached the house, some big drops of rain had fallen.

7마일(1마일은 약 1.6km) · 가장 가까운 · 기차역 · 전보를 치다 · (보통 6-8명이 타는) 유람 마차 · 기분 좋게, 의기양양하게 · 7월 · 저녁 · 공기, 대기 · 은은한 · 향기, 냄새 · 소나무 · 이따금씩, 가끔 · 산비둘기 · …에 대해 곰곰이 생각하다 · 달콤한 · 목소리 · 바스락거리는 · 양치식물 · 광이 나는, 윤기 있는 · 가슴 · 꿩 · 다람쥐 · 엿보다 · 너도밤나무 · 지나가다 · 토끼 · 획획 지나가다 · 덤불숲 · 이끼로 뒤덮인 · 둔덕 · 꼬리 · 들어가다, 입장하다 · (도시의) 거리, □가 · 갑자기 · 구름 · 기묘한, 이상한 · 고요, 정적 · (지구의) 대기, 공기 · 떼까마귀 · 조용히 · 닿다, 도착하다 · 방울

Standing on the steps to receive them was an old woman, neatly dressed in black silk, with a white cap and apron. This was Mrs. Umney, the housekeeper, whom Mrs. Otis, at Lady Canterville's earnest request, had consented to keep in her former position. She made them each a low curtsey as they alighted, and said in a quaint, old-fashioned manner, "I bid you welcome to Canterville Chase."

Following her, they passed through the fine Tudor hall into the library, a long, low room, panelled in black oak, at the end of which was a large stained glass window. Here they found tea laid out for them, and, after taking off their wraps, they sat down and began to look round, while Mrs. Umney waited on them.

Suddenly Mrs. Otis caught sight of a dull red stain on the floor just by the fireplace, and, quite unconscious of what it really signified, said to Mrs. Umney, "I am afraid something has been spilt there."

"Yes, madam," replied the old housekeeper in a low voice, "blood has been spilt on that spot."

"How horrid!" cried Mrs. Otis; "I don't at all care for blood-stains in a sitting-room. It must be removed at once."

The old woman smiled, and answered in the same low, mysterious voice, "It is the blood of Lady Eleanore de Canterville, who was murdered on that very spot by her own husband, Sir Simon de Canterville, in 1575. Sir Simon survived her nine years, and disappeared suddenly under very mysterious circumstances. His body has never been discovered, but his guilty spirit still haunts the Chase. The blood-stain has been much admired by tourists and others, and cannot be removed."

"That is all nonsense," cried Washington Otis; "Pinkerton's Champion Stain Remover and Paragon Detergent will clean it up in no time," and before the terrified housekeeper could interfere, he had fallen upon his knees, and was rapidly scouring the floor with a small stick of what looked like a black cosmetic. In a few moments no trace of the blood-stain could be seen.

"I knew Pinkerton would do it," he exclaimed, triumphantly, as he looked round at his admiring family; but no sooner had he said these words than a terrible flash of lightning lit up the sombre room, a fearful peal of thunder made them all start to their feet, and Mrs. Umney fainted.

"What a monstrous climate!" said the American Minister, calmly, as he lit a long cheroot. "I guess the old country is so overpopulated that they have not enough decent weather for everybody. I have always been of opinion that emigration is the only thing for England."

"My dear Hiram," cried Mrs. Otis, "what can we do with a woman who faints?"

"Charge it to her like breakages," answered the Minister; "she won't faint after that;" and in a few moments Mrs. Umney certainly came to. There was no doubt, however, that she was extremely upset, and she sternly warned Mr. Otis to beware of some trouble coming to the house.

"I have seen things with my own eyes, sir," she said, "that would make any Christian's hair stand on end, and many and many a night I have not closed my eyes in sleep for the awful things that are done here."

Mr. Otis, however, and his wife warmly assured the honest soul that they were not afraid of ghosts, and, after invoking the blessings of Providence on her new master and mistress, and making arrangements for an increase of salary, the old housekeeper tottered off to her own room.

2

The storm raged fiercely all that night, but nothing of particular note occurred.

The next morning, however, when they came down to breakfast, they found the terrible stain of blood once again on the floor.

"I don't think it can be the fault of the Para-gon Detergent," said Washington, "for I have tried it with everything. It must be the ghost."

He accordingly rubbed out the stain a second time, but the second morning it appeared again. The third morning also it was there, though the library had been locked up at night by Mr. Otis himself, and the key carried up-stairs.

The whole family were now quite interested;
Mr. Otis began to suspect that he had been too
dogmatic in his denial of the existence of ghosts,
Mrs. Otis expressed her intention of joining the
Psychical Society, and Washington prepared a
long letter to Messrs. Myers and Podmore on
the subject of the Permanence of Sanguineous
Stains when connected with Crime. That night
all doubts about the objective existence of phan-
tasmata were removed for ever.

The day had been warm and sunny; and, in
the cool of the evening, the whole family went
out to drive. They did not return home till nine
o'clock, when they had a light supper.

The conversation in no way turned upon
ghosts, so there were not even those primary
conditions of receptive expectations which so
often precede the presentation of psychical phenomena.

The subjects discussed, as I have since
learned from Mr. Otis, were merely such as form

the ordinary conversation of cultured Ameri-cans of the better class, such as the immense superiority of Miss Fanny Devonport over Sarah Bernhardt as an actress; the difficulty of obtain-ing green corn, buckwheat cakes, and hominy, even in the best English houses; the importance of Boston in the development of the world-soul; the advantages of the baggage-check system in railway travelling; and the sweetness of the New York accent as compared to the London drawl. No mention at all was made of the supernat-ural, nor was Sir Simon de Canterville alluded to in any way.

At eleven o'clock the family retired, and by half-past all the lights were out. Some time af-ter, Mr. Otis was awakened by a curious noise in the corridor, outside his room. It sounded like the clank of metal, and seemed to be coming nearer every moment. He got up at once, struck a match, and looked at the time. It was exactly one o'clock.

He was quite calm, and felt his pulse, which
차분한, 침착한   맥박, 맥
was not at all feverish. The strange noise still
열이 나는, 몹시 흥분한   이상한, 낯선   소음
continued, and with it he heard distinctly the
(쉬지 않고) 계속되다   뚜렷하게, 명백하게
sound of footsteps. He put on his slippers, took
발자국   슬리퍼를 신다
a small oblong phial out of his dressing-case,
직사각형의, 길쭉한   작은 유리병
and opened the door.

Right in front of him he saw, in the wan
~앞에   창백한, 파리한
moonlight, an old man of terrible aspect. His
달빛   측면, 양상, 모습
eyes were as red burning coals; long grey hair
불타는, 불 붙은 석탄   회색의, 잿빛의
fell over his shoulders in matted coils; his
어깨   엉겨[들러] 붙은   고리, 사리
garments, which were of antique cut, were
의복, 옷   골동품
soiled and ragged, and from his wrists and
더러운   누더기가 된, 다 해진   손목, 팔목
ankles hung heavy manacles and rusty gyves.
발목   무거운   수갑, 족쇄   녹슨   차꼬, 수갑
"My dear sir," said Mr. Otis, "I really must
정말로, 실제로
insist on your oiling those chains, and have
(…해야 한다고) 고집하다[주장하다/우기다]
brought you for that purpose a small bottle of
목적, 용도   병
the Tammany Rising Sun Lubricator. It is said
to be completely efficacious upon one applica-
완벽하게, 철저하게   효과적인 (=effective)   바르기, 도포
tion, and there are several testimonials to that
몇몇의, 여럿의 (품질에 대한) 추천의 글
effect on the wrapper from some of our most
영향; 결과, 효과
eminent native divines. I shall leave it here for
저명한

you by the bedroom candles, and will be happy
to supply you with more, should you require it."

With these words the United States Minister laid the bottle down on a marble table, and,
closing his door, retired to rest.

For a moment the Canterville ghost stood
quite motionless in natural indignation; then,
dashing the bottle violently upon the polished
floor, he fled down the corridor, uttering hollow
groans, and emitting a ghastly green light.

Just, however, as he reached the top of
the great oak staircase, a door was flung open,
two little white-robed figures appeared, and a
large pillow whizzed past his head! There was
evidently no time to be lost, so, hastily adopting
the Fourth dimension of Space as a means of escape, he vanished through the wainscoting, and
the house became quite quiet.

On reaching a small secret chamber in the
left wing, he leaned up against a moonbeam to
recover his breath, and began to try and realize

his position. Never, in a brilliant and uninter-
rupted career of three hundred years, had he
been so grossly insulted.

He thought of the Dowager Duchess, whom
he had frightened into a fit as she stood before
the glass in her lace and diamonds; of the four
housemaids, who had gone into hysterics when
he merely grinned at them through the curtains
on one of the spare bedrooms; of the rector of
the parish, whose candle he had blown out as
he was coming late one night from the library,
and who had been under the care of Sir Wil-
liam Gull ever since, a perfect martyr to nervous
disorders; and of old Madame de Tremouillac,
who, having wakened up one morning early and
seen a skeleton seated in an armchair by the fire
reading her diary, had been confined to her bed
for six weeks with an attack of brain fever, and,
on her recovery, had become reconciled to the
Church, and broken off her connection with that
notorious sceptic, Monsieur de Voltaire.

146

He remembered the terrible night when the wicked Lord Canterville was found choking in his dressing-room, with the knave of diamonds half-way down his throat, and confessed, just before he died, that he had cheated Charles James Fox out of £50,000 at Crockford's by means of that very card, and swore that the ghost had made him swallow it.

remembered 기억하다, 생각해 내다 · terrible 끔찍한, 지독한, 무시무시한 · wicked 사악한, 못된 · choking 숨이 막히다, 질식시키다 · dressing-room (침실 옆에 딸린) 옷방 · knave of diamonds 다이아몬드 잭 카드 · throat 목구멍 · confessed 자백하다, 고백하다 · died 죽다 · cheated 속이다, 기만하다 · swore 맹세하다(swear의 과거) · swallow 삼키다, (목구멍으로) 넘기다

All his great achievements came back to him again, from the butler who had shot himself in the pantry because he had seen a green hand tapping at the window-pane, to the beautiful Lady Stutfield, who was always obliged to wear a black velvet band round her throat to hide the mark of five fingers burnt upon her white skin, and who drowned herself at last in the carp-pond at the end of the King's Walk.

achievements 업적, 성취한 것 · butler 집사 · shot 쏘다 · pantry 식료품 저장실 · tapping 두드리다 · window-pane 창유리, 유리창 · obliged 부득이 …하게 하다 · throat 목 · hide 감추다, 가리다 · fingers 손가락 · burnt 불탄 · drowned 물에 빠져 죽다, 익사하다 · at last 마침내, 결국 · carp-pond 잉어 연못

With the enthusiastic egotism of the true artist, he went over his most celebrated perfor-mances, and smiled bitterly to himself as he re-called to mind his last appearance as "Red Reu-

enthusiastic 열렬한, 열광적인 · egotism 이기주의, 자기 본위 · artist 예술가 · celebrated 유명한, 기념할 만한 · bitterly 비통하게, 쓰라리게 · appearance 출현, 모습을 보임

ben, or the Strangled Babe," his début as "Guant Gibeon, the Blood-sucker of Bexley Moor," and the furore he had excited one lovely June evening by merely playing ninepins with his own bones upon the lawn-tennis ground.

And after all this some wretched modern Americans were to come and offer him the Rising Sun Lubricator, and throw pillows at his head! It was quite unbearable. Besides, no ghost in history had ever been treated in this manner. Accordingly, he determined to have vengeance, and remained till daylight in an attitude of deep thought.

3

The next morning, when the Otis family met at breakfast, they discussed the ghost at some length.

The United States Minister was naturally a little annoyed to find that his present had not been accepted.

"I have no wish," he said, "to do the ghost any personal injury, and I must say that, considering the length of time he has been in the house, I don't think it is at all polite to throw pillows at him,"—a very just remark, at which, I am sorry to say, the twins burst into shouts of laughter.

"Upon the other hand," he continued, "if he really declines to use the Rising Sun Lubricator, we shall have to take his chains from him. It would be quite impossible to sleep, with such a noise going on outside the bedrooms."

For the rest of the week, however, they were undisturbed, the only thing that excited any attention being the continual renewal of the blood-stain on the library floor.

This certainly was very strange, as the door was always locked at night by Mr. Otis, and the windows kept closely barred. The chameleon-like colour, also, of the stain excited a good deal of comment.

Some mornings it was a dull (almost Indian) red, then it would be vermilion, then a rich purple, and once when they came down for family prayers, according to the simple rites of the Free American Reformed Episcopalian Church, they found it a bright emerald-green.

These kaleidoscopic changes naturally

amused the party very much, and bets on the
즐겁게[미소 짓게/재미있게] 하다   돈을 걸다, 내기를 하다
subject were freely made every evening.
주제, 문제, 사안

The only person who did not enter into the
사람   들어오다, 입장하다
joke was little Virginia, who, for some unex-
농담, 장난   설명할 수 없는
plained reason, was always a good deal dis-
이유, 근거   괴롭히다
tressed at the sight of the blood-stain, and very
광경, 장면
nearly cried the morning it was emerald-green.
거의   울다

The second appearance of the ghost was on
출현, 나타남
Sunday night. Shortly after they had gone to bed
얼마 안 되어, 곧
they were suddenly alarmed by a fearful crash
갑자기   놀라게 하다   무시무시한   요란한 소리
in the hall.

Rushing down-stairs, they found that a large
아래층
suit of old armour had become detached from
갑옷   떼다[분리하다], 분리되다
its stand, and had fallen on the stone floor, while
돌바닥
seated in a high-backed chair was the Canter-
등받이가 높은 의자
ville ghost, rubbing his knees with an expression
문지르다   무릎   표정
of acute agony on his face.
극심한[극도의] 고통   얼굴

The twins, having brought their pea-shoot-
ers with them, at once discharged two pellets on
him, with that accuracy of aim which can only
be attained by long and careful practice on a
writing-master, while the United States Minister
covered him with his revolver, and called upon
him, in accordance with Californian etiquette, to
hold up his hands!

The ghost started up with a wild shriek
of rage, and swept through them like a mist,
extinguishing Washington Otis's candle as he
passed, and so leaving them all in total darkness. On reaching the top of the staircase he
recovered himself, and determined to give his
celebrated peal of demoniac laughter. This he
had on more than one occasion found extremely
useful. It was said to have turned Lord Raker's
wig grey in a single night, and had certainly
made three of Lady Canterville's French govern-
esses give warning before their month was up.
He accordingly laughed his most horrible

laugh, till the old vaulted roof rang and rang again, but hardly had the fearful echo died away when a door opened, and Mrs. Otis came out in a light blue dressing-gown.

"I am afraid you are far from well," she said, "and have brought you a bottle of Doctor Dobell's tincture. If it is indigestion, you will find it a most excellent remedy."

The ghost glared at her in fury, and began at once to make preparations for turning himself into a large black dog, an accomplishment for which he was justly renowned, and to which the family doctor always attributed the permanent idiocy of Lord Canterville's uncle, the Hon. Thomas Horton.

The sound of approaching footsteps, however, made him hesitate in his fell purpose, so he contented himself with becoming faintly phosphorescent, and vanished with a deep churchyard groan, just as the twins had come up to him.

On reaching his room he entirely broke down, and became a prey to the most violent agitation. The vulgarity of the twins, and the gross materialism of Mrs. Otis, were naturally extremely annoying, but what really distressed him most was that he had been unable to wear the suit of mail.

He had hoped that even modern Americans would be thrilled by the sight of a Spectre in armour, if for no more sensible reason, at least out of respect for their natural poet Longfellow, over whose graceful and attractive poetry he himself had whiled away many a weary hour when the Cantervilles were up in town.

Besides it was his own suit. He had worn it with great success at the Kenilworth tournament, and had been highly complimented on it by no less a person than the Virgin Queen herself.

Yet when he had put it on, he had been completely overpowered by the weight of the huge

breastplate and steel casque, and had fallen
heavily on the stone pavement, barking both his
knees severely, and bruising the knuckles of his
right hand.

For some days after this he was extremely ill,
and hardly stirred out of his room at all, except
to keep the blood-stain in proper repair.
However, by taking great care of himself, he
recovered, and resolved to make a third attempt
to frighten the United States Minister and his
family.

He selected Friday, August 17th, for his appearance, and spent most of that day in looking over his wardrobe, ultimately deciding in
favour of a large slouched hat with a red feather,
a winding-sheet frilled at the wrists and neck,
and a rusty dagger. Towards evening a violent
storm of rain came on, and the wind was so
high that all the windows and doors in the old
house shook and rattled. In fact, it was just such
weather as he loved.

His plan of action was this. He was to make his way quietly to Washington Otis's room, gibber at him from the foot of the bed, and stab himself three times in the throat to the sound of low music. He bore Washington a special grudge, being quite aware that it was he who was in the habit of removing the famous Canterville blood-stain by means of Pinkerton's Paragon Detergent.

Having reduced the reckless and foolhardy youth to a condition of abject terror, he was then to proceed to the room occupied by the United States Minister and his wife, and there to place a clammy hand on Mrs. Otis's forehead, while he hissed into her trembling husband's ear the awful secrets of the charnel-house. With regard to little Virginia, he had not quite made up his mind. She had never insulted him in any way, and was pretty and gentle. A few hollow groans from the wardrobe, he thought, would be more than sufficient, or, if

that failed to wake her, he might grabble at the counterpane with palsy-twitching fingers.

As for the twins, he was quite determined to teach them a lesson. The first thing to be done was, of course, to sit upon their chests, so as to produce the stifling sensation of nightmare. Then, as their beds were quite close to each other, to stand between them in the form of a green, icy-cold corpse, till they became para- lyzed with fear, and finally, to throw off the winding-sheet, and crawl round the room, with white, bleached bones and one rolling eyeball, in the character of "Dumb Daniel, or the Suicide's Skeleton," a rôle in which he had on more than one occasion produced a great effect, and which he considered quite equal to his famous part of "Martin the Maniac, or the Masked Mystery."

At half-past ten he heard the family going to bed. For some time he was disturbed by wild shrieks of laughter from the twins, who, with the light-hearted gaiety of schoolboys, were evidently amusing themselves before they retired to rest, but at a quarter-past eleven all was still, and, as midnight sounded, he sallied forth. The owl beat against the window-panes, the raven croaked from the old yew-tree, and the wind wandered moaning round the house like a lost soul; but the Otis family slept unconscious of their doom, and high above the rain and storm he could hear the steady snoring of the Minister for the United States.

He stepped stealthily out of the wainscoting, with an evil smile on his cruel, wrinkled mouth, and the moon hid her face in a cloud as he stole past the great oriel window, where his own arms and those of his murdered wife were blazoned in azure and gold. On and on he glided, like an evil shadow, the very darkness seeming to loathe him as he passed. Once he thought he heard something call, and stopped; but it was only the baying of a dog from the Red Farm, and he went on, mut-

tering strange sixteenth-century curses, and
ever and anon brandishing the rusty dagger in
the midnight air.

Finally he reached the corner of the passage
that led to luckless Washington's room. For a
moment he paused there, the wind blowing his
long grey locks about his head, and twisting into
grotesque and fantastic folds the nameless horror of the dead man's shroud.

Then the clock struck the quarter, and he
felt the time was come. He chuckled to himself,
and turned the corner; but no sooner had he
done so than, with a piteous wail of terror, he
fell back, and hid his blanched face in his long,
bony hands. Right in front of him was standing
a horrible spectre, motionless as a carven image,
and monstrous as a madman's dream! Its head
was bald and burnished; its face round, and fat,
and white; and hideous laughter seemed to have
writhed its features into an eternal grin.

---

glosses: 이상한, 낯선 · 16세기 · 욕(설), 악담, 저주 · (무기를) 휘두르다 · 녹슨 · 단도, 단검 · 마침내 · 도착하다, 닿다 · 코너, 모퉁이 · 복도 · 불운한, 운 없는 · 잠시 · (잠깐) 멈추다 · 바람 · 불다 · 긴 · 회색의 · 머리털, 머리카락 · 비틀다, 꼬다 · 기괴한, 기이한 · 환상적인 · 주름 · 입에 담기도 끔찍한 공포 · 수의(壽衣) · (벽에 걸거나 실내에 두는) 시계 · 낄낄거리다, 킬킬 웃다 · 돌다 · 모퉁이 · 가련한 · 울부짖음, 통곡 · 공포, 두려움 · 가리다, 감추다 · 핼쑥한, 새파래진 · 뼈의, 앙상한 · ~앞에 · 유령 · 움직임 없이, 꼼짝 않고 · 조각한(= carved) · 가공할, 괴물 같은 · 미친 사람, 광인 · 대머리의 · 윤이 나다, 광택이 나다 · 둥근 · 뚱뚱한 · 흉측한, 흉물스러운, 끔찍한 · 온몸을 비틀다 · 이목구비(의 각 부분) · 영원한 · 활짝 웃음

From the eyes streamed rays of scarlet light,
흘러나오다   빛, 광선   주홍색의

the mouth was a wide well of fire, and a hideous
넓은   우물

garment, like to his own, swathed with its silent
의복, 옷   감싸다, 뒤덮다

snows the Titan form.
타이탄 같은 사람

On its breast was a placard with strange
가슴   플래카드, 현수막, 펼침막

writing in antique characters, some scroll of
고대의   글씨, 글자, 부호   두루마리

shame it seemed, some record of wild sins,
수치심   기록   죄

some awful calendar of crime, and, with its right
끔찍한   기록부   범죄

hand, it bore aloft a falchion of gleaming steel.
하늘[위로] 높이   언월도(偃月刀)   빛나는   강철

Never having seen a ghost before, he nat-
유령   당연히

urally was terribly frightened, and, after a sec-
끔찍하게, 혹독하게

ond hasty glance at the awful phantom, he
흘깃[휙] 보다   유령, 혼령

fled back to his room, tripping up in his long
달아나다, 도망치다   실수하다, 다리를 걸다

winding-sheet as he sped down the corridor,
빨리 가다(speed의 과거, 과거분사)

and finally dropping the rusty dagger into the
마침내   떨어뜨리다   녹슨   단도, 단검

Minister's jack-boots, where it was found in the
잭 부츠(무릎까지 올라오는 장화)

morning by the butler.
집사

Once in the privacy of his own apartment, he
사생활[프라이버시]

flung himself down on a small pallet-bed, and
내던지다(fling의 과거, 과거분사)   짚으로 만든 침대

hid his face under the clothes. After a time, how-
옷, 의복

ever, the brave old Canterville spirit asserted
용감한   영혼, 정신   주장하다

itself, and he determined to go and speak to the other ghost as soon as it was daylight.

Accordingly, just as the dawn was touching the hills with silver, he returned towards the spot where he had first laid eyes on the grisly phantom, feeling that, after all, two ghosts were better than one, and that, by the aid of his new friend, he might safely grapple with the twins.

On reaching the spot, however, a terrible sight met his gaze. Something had evidently happened to the spectre, for the light had entirely faded from its hollow eyes, the gleaming falchion had fallen from its hand, and it was leaning up against the wall in a strained and uncomfortable attitude. He rushed forward and seized it in his arms, when, to his horror, the head slipped off and rolled on the floor, the body assumed a recumbent posture, and he found himself clasping a white dimity bed-curtain, with a sweeping-brush, a kitchen cleaver, and a hollow turnip lying at his feet!

Unable to understand this curious transfor-
이해하다   별난, 특이한, 기이한 변화, 변신

mation, he clutched the placard with feverish
(꽉) 움켜잡다   몹시 흥분한, 과열된

haste, and there, in the grey morning light, he

read these fearful words:—
무서운, 끔찍한, 두려운

YE OTIS GHOSTE
= the ((옛글투))

Ye Onlie True and Originale Spook,
= only 진실, 진짜   원래[본래]의   유령, 귀신

Beware of Ye Imitationes.
…에 주의하라   모조품

All others are counterfeite.
위조의, 모조의

The whole thing flashed across him. He had
전체의, 전부의   (생각 따위가) 퍼뜩 떠오르다

been tricked, foiled, and out-witted! The old
속이다   좌절시키다, 저지하다 …보다 한 수 앞서다

Canterville look came into his eyes; he ground
갈다

his toothless gums together; and, raising his
이 없는   잇몸   들어 올리다

withered hands high above his head, swore ac-
시들다, 말라 죽다   맹세하다

cording to the picturesque phraseology of the
그림 같은, 생생한   어법

antique school, that, when Chanticleer had
〈캔터버리 이야기〉에 나오는 수탉

sounded twice his merry horn, deeds of blood
2번   즐거운   나팔   행위, 행동

would be wrought, and murder walk abroad
초래하다, 일으키다   살인

with silent feet. Hardly had he finished this
끝내다, 마치다

awful oath when, from the red-tiled roof of a distant homestead, a cock crew. He laughed a long, low, bitter laugh, and waited. Hour after hour he waited, but the cock, for some strange reason, did not crow again.

Finally, at half-past seven, the arrival of the housemaids made him give up his fearful vigil, and he stalked back to his room, thinking of his vain oath and baffled purpose. There he consulted several books of ancient chivalry, of which he was exceedingly fond, and found that, on every occasion on which this oath had been used, Chanticleer had always crowed a second time.

"Perdition seize the naughty fowl," he muttered, "I have seen the day when, with my stout spear, I would have run him through the gorge, and made him crow for me an 'twere in death!"

He then retired to a comfortable lead coffin, and stayed there till evening.

4

The next day the ghost was very weak and tired. The terrible excitement of the last four weeks was beginning to have its effect. His nerves were completely shattered, and he started at the slightest noise.

For five days he kept his room, and at last made up his mind to give up the point of the blood-stain on the library floor. If the Otis family did not want it, they clearly did not deserve it. They were evidently people on a low, material plane of existence, and quite incapable of appreciating the symbolic value of sensuous phenomena.

The question of phantasmic apparitions, and
the development of astral bodies, was of course
quite a different matter, and really not under his
control.

It was his solemn duty to appear in the corridor once a week, and to gibber from the large
oriel window on the first and third Wednesdays
in every month, and he did not see how he could
honourably escape from his obligations.
It is quite true that his life had been very
evil, but, upon the other hand, he was most
conscientious in all things connected with the
supernatural.
For the next three Saturdays, accordingly,
he traversed the corridor as usual between
midnight and three o'clock, taking every possible precaution against being either heard or
seen. He removed his boots, trod as lightly as
possible on the old worm-eaten boards, wore a
large black velvet cloak, and was careful to use
the Rising Sun Lubricator for oiling his chains.

I am bound to acknowledge that it was with a good deal of difficulty that he brought himself to adopt this last mode of protection.

However, one night, while the family were at dinner, he slipped into Mr. Otis's bedroom and carried off the bottle. He felt a little humiliated at first, but afterwards was sensible enough to see that there was a great deal to be said for the invention, and, to a certain degree, it served his purpose.

Still in spite of everything he was not left unmolested. Strings were continually being stretched across the corridor, over which he tripped in the dark, and on one occasion, while dressed for the part of "Black Isaac, or the Huntsman of Hogley Woods," he met with a severe fall, through treading on a butter-slide, which the twins had constructed from the en-trance of the Tapestry Chamber to the top of the oak staircase.

This last insult so enraged him, that he resolved to make one final effort to assert his dignity and social position, and determined to visit the insolent young Etonians the next night in his celebrated character of "Reckless Rupert, or the Headless Earl."

He had not appeared in this disguise for more than seventy years; in fact, not since he had so frightened pretty Lady Barbara Modish by means of it, that she suddenly broke off her engagement with the present Lord Canterville's grandfather, and ran away to Gretna Green with handsome Jack Castletown, declaring that nothing in the world would induce her to marry into a family that allowed such a horrible phantom to walk up and down the terrace at twilight. Poor Jack was afterwards shot in a duel by Lord Canterville on Wandsworth Common, and Lady Barbara died of a broken heart at Tunbridge Wells before the year was out, so, in every way, it had been a great success.

It was, however an extremely difficult "make-up," if I may use such a theatrical expression in connection with one of the greatest mysteries of the supernatural, or, to employ a more scientific term, the higher-natural world, and it took him fully three hours to make his preparations.

At last everything was ready, and he was very pleased with his appearance. The big leather riding-boots that went with the dress were just a little too large for him, and he could only find one of the two horse-pistols, but, on the whole, he was quite satisfied, and at a quarter-past one he glided out of the wainscoting and crept down the corridor.

On reaching the room occupied by the twins, which I should mention was called the Blue Bed Chamber, on account of the colour of its hangings, he found the door just ajar. Wishing to make an effective entrance, he flung it wide open, when a heavy jug of water fell right down on him, wetting him to the skin,

and just missing his left shoulder by a couple
of inches. At the same moment he heard stifled
shrieks of laughter proceeding from the four-
post bed.

The shock to his nervous system was so
great that he fled back to his room as hard as he
could go, and the next day he was laid up with a
severe cold. The only thing that at all consoled
him in the whole affair was the fact that he had
not brought his head with him, for, had he done
so, the consequences might have been very seri-
ous.

He now gave up all hope of ever frightening
this rude American family, and contented himself, as a rule, with creeping about the passages
in list slippers, with a thick red muffler round
his throat for fear of draughts, and a small
arquebuse, in case he should be attacked by the
twins.

The final blow he received occurred on the
19th of September. He had gone down-stairs to

the great entrance-hall, feeling sure that there, at any rate, he would be quite unmolested, and was amusing himself by making satirical remarks on the large Saroni photographs of the United States Minister and his wife which had now taken the place of the Canterville family pictures.

He was simply but neatly clad in a long shroud, spotted with churchyard mould, had tied up his jaw with a strip of yellow linen, and carried a small lantern and a sexton's spade. In fact, he was dressed for the character of "Jonas the Graveless, or the Corpse-Snatcher of Chertsey Barn," one of his most remarkable impersonations, and one which the Cantervilles had every reason to remember, as it was the real origin of their quarrel with their neighbour, Lord Rufford.

It was about a quarter-past two o'clock in the morning, and, as far as he could ascertain, no one was stirring.

As he was strolling towards the library, how-
거닐다, 산책하다 ~쪽으로
ever, to see if there were any traces left of the
흔적, 자취 남다
blood-stain, suddenly there leaped out on him
핏자국 갑자기 펄쩍 뛰어나오다
from a dark corner two figures, who waved their
어두운 구석, 모퉁이 형체, 모습 흔들다
arms wildly above their heads, and shrieked out
거칠게, 사납게 새된 소리를 지르다
"BOO!" in his ear.

Seized with a panic, which, under the cir-
극심한 공포, 공황 환경, 상황, 정황
cumstances, was only natural, he rushed for the
돌진하다, 급히 달려가다
staircase, but found Washington Otis waiting
~을 기다리다
for him there with the big garden-syringe, and
정원용 펌프
being thus hemmed in by his enemies on ev-
~을 (꼼짝 못하게) 둘러싸다 적
ery side, and driven almost to bay, he vanished
거의 사라지다
into the great iron stove, which, fortunately for
쇠, 철 난로 다행히, 운 좋게도
him, was not lit, and had to make his way home
light의 과거, 과거분사
through the flues and chimneys, arriving at his
(굴뚝의) 연통, 연관 굴뚝
own room in a terrible state of dirt, disorder,
지독한, 끔찍한 먼지, 때 엉망, 어수선함
and despair.
절망

After this he was not seen again on any nocturnal expedition. The twins lay in wait for him on several occasions, and strewed the passages with nutshells every night to the great annoyance of their parents and the servants, but it was of no avail. It was quite evident that his feelings were so wounded that he would not appear. Mr. Otis consequently resumed his great work on the history of the Democratic Party, on which he had been engaged for some years; Mrs. Otis organized a wonderful clam-bake, which amazed the whole county; the boys took to lacrosse, euchre, poker, and other American national games, and Virginia rode about the lanes on her pony, accompanied by the young Duke of Cheshire, who had come to spend the last week of his holidays at Canterville Chase. It was generally assumed that the ghost had gone away, and, in fact, Mr. Otis wrote a letter to that effect to Lord Canterville, who, in reply, expressed his great pleasure at the news, and

sent his best congratulations to the Minister's
worthy wife.

The Otises, however, were deceived, for the ghost was still in the house, and though now almost an invalid, was by no means ready to let matters rest, particularly as he heard that among the guests was the young Duke of Cheshire, whose grand-uncle, Lord Francis Stilton, had once bet a hundred guineas with Colonel Carbury that he would play dice with the Canterville ghost, and was found the next morning lying on the floor of the card-room in such a helpless paralytic state that, though he lived on to a great age, he was never able to say anything again but "Double Sixes."

The story was well known at the time, though, of course, out of respect to the feelings of the two noble families, every attempt was made to hush it up, and a full account of all the circumstances connected with it will be found in the third volume of Lord Tattle's Recollections

of the Prince Regent and his Friends.

The ghost, then, was naturally very anxious to show that he had not lost his influence over the Stiltons, with whom, indeed, he was distantly connected, his own first cousin having been married en secondes noces to the Sieur de Bulkeley, from whom, as every one knows, the Dukes of Cheshire are lineally descended.

Accordingly, he made arrangements for appearing to Virginia's little lover in his celebrated impersonation of "The Vampire Monk, or the Bloodless Benedictine," a performance so horrible that when old Lady Startup saw it, which she did on one fatal New Year's Eve, in the year 1764, she went off into the most piercing shrieks, which culminated in violent apoplexy, and died in three days, after disinheriting the Cantervilles, who were her nearest relations, and leaving all her money to her London apothecary.

At the last moment, however, his terror of the twins prevented his leaving his room, and

the little Duke slept in peace under the great
평화롭게
feathered canopy in the Royal Bedchamber, and
(침대 위에 지붕처럼 늘어뜨린) 덮개
dreamed of Virginia.

5

A few days after this, Virginia and her curly-haired cavalier went out riding on
곡슬머리의   왕당파
Brockley meadows, where she tore her habit so
초원, 목초지   찢어지다   의복
badly in getting through a hedge that, on their
생울타리, 산울타리
return home, she made up her mind to go up by
귀환   결심하다, 결정하다
the back staircase so as not to be seen.
뒤쪽 층계

As she was running past the Tapestry Cham-
지나가다
ber, the door of which happened to be open, she

fancied she saw some one inside, and thinking
생각[상상]하다   안에, 내부에
it was her mother's maid, who sometimes used
하녀   때때로, 가끔
to bring her work there, looked in to ask her to
요청하다, 부탁하다
mend her habit. To her immense surprise, how-
꿰매다, 수선하다   너무나 놀랍게도, 어마어마하게 깜짝 놀랍게도
ever, it was the Canterville Ghost himself!

He was sitting by the window, watching the ruined gold of the yellowing trees fly through the air, and the red leaves dancing madly down the long avenue. His head was leaning on his hand, and his whole attitude was one of extreme depression.

Indeed, so forlorn, and so much out of repair did he look, that little Virginia, whose first idea had been to run away and lock herself in her room, was filled with pity, and determined to try and comfort him.

So light was her footfall, and so deep his melancholy, that he was not aware of her presence till she spoke to him.

"I am so sorry for you," she said, "but my brothers are going back to Eton to-morrow, and then, if you behave yourself, no one will annoy you."

"It is absurd asking me to behave myself," he answered, looking round in astonishment at the pretty little girl who had ventured to address

183

him, "quite absurd. I must rattle my chains, [덜컹[달그락]거리다] and groan [신음[끙 하는] 소리를 내다] through keyholes, [열쇠구멍] and walk about [이리저리 돌아다니다] at night, if that is what you mean. It is my only reason for existing." [뜻하다, 의미하다 / 이유, 근거 / 존재, 실재, 현존]

"It is no reason at all for existing, and you know you have been very wicked. [사악한, 악랄한] Mrs. Umney told us, the first day we arrived here, that you [도착하다] had killed your wife." [죽이다]

"Well, I quite admit it," [인정[시인]하다 (=confess)] said the Ghost, petu-lantly, [안달하여, 성마르게] "but it was a purely family matter, and [순전히, 전적으로, 오직] concerned no one else." [영향을 미치다, 관련되다, 걱정하다]

"It is very wrong to kill any one," [잘못된, 틀린] said Vir-ginia, who at times had a sweet puritan gravity, [달콤한 / 청교도의 / 엄숙함] caught from some old New England ancestor. [조상, 선조]

"Oh, I hate the cheap severity of abstract [몹시 싫어하다[질색하다] / 엄격함, 통렬함 / 관념적인, 추상적인] ethics! My wife was very plain, never had my [윤리, 도덕 / 평범한, 아름답지 않은, 매력 없는] ruffs properly starched, and knew nothing about [주름 칼라[옷깃] / (옷, 시트에) 풀을 먹이다] cookery. Why, there was a buck I had shot in [요리(법) / 수사슴, 수토끼] Hogley Woods, a magnificent pricket, and do [참으로 아름다운 / 두 살 난 수사슴] you know how she had it sent to table? How-ever, it is no matter now, for it is all over, and [끝나다]

I don't think it was very nice of her brothers to
잘한, 괜찮은
starve me to death, though I did kill her."
굶기다, 굶겨 죽이다   비록 ~지만[~라 해도]
        "Starve you to death? Oh, Mr. Ghost—I
mean Sir Simon, are you hungry? I have a sand-
뜻하다, 의미하다   배고픈, 굶주린
wich in my case. Would you like it?"

        "No, thank you, I never eat anything now;
                              먹다
but it is very kind of you, all the same, and you
                    친절한, 온화한
are much nicer than the rest of your horrid,
~보다 좋은[멋진, 훌륭한]   진저리나는, 지독한
rude, vulgar, dishonest family."
무례한   저속한, 천박한   정직하지 않은
        "Stop!" cried Virginia, stamping her foot, "it
                                발을 구르다
is you who are rude, and horrid, and vulgar, and
              무례한   진저리나는   저속한, 천박한
as for dishonesty, you know you stole the paints
        불성실한, 부정직한   훔치다
out of my box to try and furbish up that ridicu-
                              새롭게 하다   웃기는, 말도 안 되는
lous blood-stain in the library. First you took all
      핏자국   서재
my reds, including the vermilion, and I couldn't
              …을 포함하여   주홍색
do any more sunsets, then you took the emer-
              석양
ald-green and the chrome-yellow, and finally I
                    크롬 황색   결국
had nothing left but indigo and Chinese white,
and could only do moonlight scenes, which are
                          달빛   장면
always depressing to look at, and not at all easy
          우울한   쉬운
to paint. I never told on you, though I was very

185

much annoyed, and it was most ridiculous, the whole thing; for who ever heard of emerald-green blood?"

"Well, really," said the Ghost, rather meekly, "what was I to do? It is a very difficult thing to get real blood nowadays, and, as your brother began it all with his Paragon Detergent, I certainly saw no reason why I should not have your paints. As for colour, that is always a matter of taste: the Cantervilles have blue blood, for instance, the very bluest in England; but I know you Americans don't care for things of this kind."

"You know nothing about it, and the best thing you can do is to emigrate and improve your mind. My father will be only too happy to give you a free passage, and though there is a heavy duty on spirits of every kind, there will be no difficulty about the Custom House, as the officers are all Democrats. Once in New York, you are sure to be a great success. I know lots of people there who would give a hundred thousand dollars to have a grandfather, and much more than that to have a family ghost."

"I don't think I should like America."

"I suppose because we have no ruins and no curiosities," said Virginia, satirically.

"No ruins! no curiosities!" answered the Ghost; "you have your navy and your manners."

"Good evening; I will go and ask papa to get the twins an extra week's holiday."

"Please don't go, Miss Virginia," he cried; "I am so lonely and so unhappy, and I really don't know what to do. I want to go to sleep and I cannot."

"That's quite absurd! You have merely to go to bed and blow out the candle. It is very difficult sometimes to keep awake, especially at church, but there is no difficulty at all about sleeping. Why, even babies know how to do that, and they are not very clever."

"I have not slept for three hundred years," he said sadly, and Virginia's beautiful blue eyes

opened in wonder; "for three hundred years I
have not slept, and I am so tired."

Virginia grew quite grave, and her little lips
trembled like rose-leaves. She came towards
him, and kneeling down at his side, looked up
into his old withered face.

"Poor, poor Ghost," she murmured; "have
you no place where you can sleep?"

"Far away beyond the pine-woods," he answered, in a low, dreamy voice, "there is a little
garden. There the grass grows long and deep,
there are the great white stars of the hemlock
flower, there the nightingale sings all night long.
All night long he sings, and the cold crystal
moon looks down, and the yew-tree spreads out
its giant arms over the sleepers."

Virginia's eyes grew dim with tears, and she
hid her face in her hands.

"You mean the Garden of Death," she whispered.

"Yes, death. Death must be so beautiful. To

lie in the soft brown earth, with the grasses waving above one's head, and listen to silence. To
have no yesterday, and no to-morrow. To forget
time, to forget life, to be at peace. You can help
me. You can open for me the portals of death's
house, for love is always with you, and love is
stronger than death is."

Virginia trembled, a cold shudder ran
through her, and for a few moments there was
silence. She felt as if she was in a terrible dream.
Then the ghost spoke again, and his voice
sounded like the sighing of the wind.

"Have you ever read the old prophecy on the
library window?"

"Oh, often," cried the little girl, looking up; "I
know it quite well. It is painted in curious black
letters, and is difficult to read. There are only six
lines:

"'When a golden girl can win
Prayer from out the lips of sin,

When the barren almond bears,
(척박한, 황량한; 열매[씨]가 안 열리는)
And a little child gives away its tears,
(눈물)
Then shall all the house be still
(고요한, 조용한)
And peace come to Canterville.'
(평화)

But I don't know what they mean."
(뜻하다, 의미하다)
"They mean," he said, sadly, "that you must
(슬프게, 서글프게)
weep with me for my sins, because I have no
(울다) (죄)
tears, and pray with me for my soul, because
(눈물) (기도하다) (영혼)
I have no faith, and then, if you have always
(믿음, 신념) (늘, 언제나)
been sweet, and good, and gentle, the angel of
(다정한, 달콤한) (착한, 선한) (온화한, 상냥한) (천사)
death will have mercy on me. You will see fear-
(자비)
ful shapes in darkness, and wicked voices will
(형태, 모습) (어둠) (사악한, 악랄한)
whisper in your ear, but they will not harm you,
(속삭이다) (귀) (해치다, 해를 입히다)
for against the purity of a little child the powers
(순수함) (힘, 권세)
of Hell cannot prevail."
(지옥) (승리하다, 이기다)
Virginia made no answer, and the ghost
(대답)
wrung his hands in wild despair as he looked
(손을 비벼대다[비틀다](RING의 과거 · 과거분사)) (절망)
down at her bowed golden head.
(고개 숙인)
Suddenly she stood up, very pale, and with a
(갑자기) (창백한)
strange light in her eyes.
(낯선, 이상한)

"I am not afraid," she said firmly, "and I will ask the angel to have mercy on you."

He rose from his seat with a faint cry of joy, and taking her hand bent over it with old-fashioned grace and kissed it. His fingers were as cold as ice, and his lips burned like fire, but Virginia did not falter, as he led her across the dusky room.

On the faded green tapestry were broidered little huntsmen. They blew their tasselled horns and with their tiny hands waved to her to go back.

"Go back! little Virginia," they cried, "go back!" but the ghost clutched her hand more tightly, and she shut her eyes against them. Horrible animals with lizard tails and goggle eyes blinked at her from the carven chimneypiece, and murmured, "Beware! little Virginia, beware! we may never see you again," but the Ghost glided on more swiftly, and Virginia did not listen.

두려운, 무서운 · 단호히, 확고히 · 부탁하다 · 자비 · 일어서다 · 희미한 · 외침 · 기쁨, 환희 · 구부리다 · 구식으로 우아하게 · 손가락 · 얼음 만큼 차가운 · 불 타다 · 불 · 불안정해지다, 흔들리다 · 이끌다 · 가로지르다 · 어스름한 · 색바랜 · 수를 놓다 · 사냥꾼 · 불다 · 술을 달아 장식한 뿔피리 · 아주 작은 · 흔들다 · 돌아가! · 꽉 붙잡다 · 단단히, 꽉 · 눈을 감다 · 무시무시한, 끔찍한 · 동물 · 도마뱀의 꼬리 · 희번덕이는 · 눈을[눈이] 깜박이다 · 벽난로 위 선반에 새겨진 · 중얼거리다 · 조심해! · 미끄러져 가다 · 신속히, 빨리

192

When they reached the end of the room he
도착하다

stopped, and muttered some words she could
중얼거리다, 웅얼거리다   말, 단어

not understand. She opened her eyes, and saw
이해하다, 알아듣다   눈을 뜨다

the wall slowly fading away like a mist, and a
벽   천천히   사라지다, 꺼지다   안개

great black cavern in front of her. A bitter cold
(큰) 동굴   혹독한, 매서운

wind swept round them, and she felt something
휘몰아치다(sweep의 과거, 과거분사)

pulling at her dress.
잡아당기다

"Quick, quick," cried the Ghost, "or it will be
빨리

too late," and in a moment the wainscoting had
늦은, 지각한   징두리벽판

closed behind them, and the Tapestry Chamber
~뒤에서

was empty.
텅 빈

6

About ten minutes later, the bell rang for tea, and, as Virginia did not come down, Mrs. Otis sent up one of the footmen to tell her. After a little time he returned and said that he could not find Miss Virginia anywhere.

As she was in the habit of going out to the garden every evening to get flowers for the dinner-table, Mrs. Otis was not at all alarmed at first, but when six o'clock struck, and Virginia did not appear, she became really agitated, and sent the boys out to look for her, while she herself and Mr. Otis searched every room in the house.

At half-past six the boys came back and said
that they could find no trace of their sister anywhere. They were all now in the greatest state of
excitement, and did not know what to do, when
Mr. Otis suddenly remembered that, some few
days before, he had given a band of gipsies per-
mission to camp in the park.

He accordingly at once set off for Blackfell
Hollow, where he knew they were, accompanied
by his eldest son and two of the farm-servants.
The little Duke of Cheshire, who was perfectly
frantic with anxiety, begged hard to be allowed
to go too, but Mr. Otis would not allow him, as
he was afraid there might be a scuffle.

On arriving at the spot, however, he found
that the gipsies had gone, and it was evident
that their departure had been rather sudden,
as the fire was still burning, and some plates
were lying on the grass. Having sent off Washington and the two men to scour the district, he
ran home, and despatched telegrams to all the

police inspectors in the county, telling them to look out for a little girl who had been kidnapped by tramps or gipsies.

He then ordered his horse to be brought round, and, after insisting on his wife and the three boys sitting down to dinner, rode off down the Ascot road with a groom. He had hardly, however, gone a couple of miles, when he heard somebody galloping after him, and, looking round, saw the little Duke coming up on his pony, with his face very flushed, and no hat.

"I'm awfully sorry, Mr. Otis," gasped out the boy, "but I can't eat any dinner as long as Virginia is lost. Please don't be angry with me; if you had let us be engaged last year, there would never have been all this trouble. You won't send me back, will you? I can't go! I won't go!"

The Minister could not help smiling at the handsome young scapegrace, and was a good deal touched at his devotion to Virginia, so leaning down from his horse, he patted him kindly

on the shoulders, and said, "Well, Cecil, if you won't go back, I suppose you must come with me, but I must get you a hat at Ascot."

"Oh, bother my hat! I want Virginia!" cried the little Duke, laughing, and they galloped on to the railway station. There Mr. Otis inquired of the station-master if any one answering to the description of Virginia had been seen on the platform, but could get no news of her. The station-master, however, wired up and down the line, and assured him that a strict watch would be kept for her, and, after having bought a hat for the little Duke from a linen-draper, who was just putting up his shutters, Mr. Otis rode off to Bexley, a village about four miles away, which he was told was a well-known haunt of the gipsies, as there was a large common next to it.

Here they roused up the rural policeman, but could get no information from him, and, after riding all over the common, they turned

their horses' heads homewards, and reached
the Chase about eleven o'clock, dead-tired and
almost heart-broken.

They found Washington and the twins waiting for them at the gate-house with lanterns, as
the avenue was very dark. Not the slightest trace
of Virginia had been discovered. The gipsies had
been caught on Brockley meadows, but she was
not with them, and they had explained their
sudden departure by saying that they had mis-
taken the date of Chorton Fair, and had gone off
in a hurry for fear they should be late.

Indeed, they had been quite distressed at
hearing of Virginia's disappearance, as they
were very grateful to Mr. Otis for having allowed
them to camp in his park, and four of their
number had stayed behind to help in the search.
The carp-pond had been dragged, and the
whole Chase thoroughly gone over, but without
any result. It was evident that, for that night at
any rate, Virginia was lost to them; and it was in

a state of the deepest depression that Mr. Otis
and the boys walked up to the house, the groom
following behind with the two horses and the
pony.

In the hall they found a group of frightened
servants, and lying on a sofa in the library was
poor Mrs. Otis, almost out of her mind with terror and anxiety, and having her forehead bathed
with eau de cologne by the old housekeeper.
Mr. Otis at once insisted on her having
something to eat, and ordered up supper for
the whole party. It was a melancholy meal, as
hardly any one spoke, and even the twins were
awestruck and subdued, as they were very fond
of their sister.

When they had finished, Mr. Otis, in spite of
the entreaties of the little Duke, ordered them
all to bed, saying that nothing more could be
done that night, and that he would telegraph in
the morning to Scotland Yard for some detec-
tives to be sent down immediately.

Just as they were passing out of the dining-room, midnight began to boom from the clock tower, and when the last stroke sounded they heard a crash and a sudden shrill cry; a dreadful peal of thunder shook the house, a strain of unearthly music floated through the air, a panel at the top of the staircase flew back with a loud noise, and out on the landing, looking very pale and white, with a little casket in her hand, stepped Virginia. In a moment they had all rushed up to her. Mrs. Otis clasped her passionately in her arms, the Duke smothered her with violent kisses, and the twins executed a wild war-dance round the group.

"Good heavens! child, where have you been?" said Mr. Otis, rather angrily, thinking that she had been playing some foolish trick on them. "Cecil and I have been riding all over the country looking for you, and your mother has been frightened to death. You must never play these practical jokes any more."

"Except on the Ghost! except on the Ghost!"
(~을) 제외하고는[외에는]
shrieked the twins, as they capered about.
(신이 나서) 뛰어다니다[깡충거리다]

"My own darling, thank God you are found;

you must never leave my side again," murmured
떠나다   옆, 곁
Mrs. Otis, as she kissed the trembling child, and
떨고 있는
smoothed the tangled gold of her hair.
반듯하게 펴다[매만지다]   헝클어진

"Papa," said Virginia, quietly, "I have been
조용히, 차분하게
with the Ghost. He is dead, and you must come
죽다
and see him. He had been very wicked, but he
사악한, 악랄한
was really sorry for all that he had done, and he
미안해 하다, 유감스러워 하다
gave me this box of beautiful jewels before he
보석 (= gem)
died."

The whole family gazed at her in mute
응시하다, 빤히 쳐다보다   아연해서, 멍해서
amazement, but she was quite grave and seri-
엄숙한, 근엄한   진지한
ous; and, turning round, she led them through
이끌다
the opening in the wainscoting down a narrow
징두리 벽판   좁은
secret corridor, Washington following with a
비밀의   복도   따라가다
lighted candle, which he had caught up from the
table.

Finally, they came to a great oak door, stud-
떡갈나무 문
ded with rusty nails. When Virginia touched
녹슨   못   만지다, 손대다

it, it swung back on its heavy hinges, and they found themselves in a little low room, with a vaulted ceiling, and one tiny grated window. Imbedded in the wall was a huge iron ring, and chained to it was a gaunt skeleton, that was stretched out at full length on the stone floor, and seemed to be trying to grasp with its long fleshless fingers an old-fashioned trencher and ewer, that were placed just out of its reach. The jug had evidently been once filled with water, as it was covered inside with green mould. There was nothing on the trencher but a pile of dust.

Virginia knelt down beside the skeleton, and, folding her little hands together, began to pray silently, while the rest of the party looked on in wonder at the terrible tragedy whose secret was now disclosed to them.

"Hallo!" suddenly exclaimed one of the twins, who had been looking out of the window to try and discover in what wing of the house

the room was situated. "Hallo! the old withered
almond-tree has blossomed. I can see the flowers quite plainly in the moonlight."

"God has forgiven him," said Virginia, gravely, as she rose to her feet, and a beautiful light
seemed to illumine her face.

"What an angel you are!" cried the young
Duke, and he put his arm round her neck, and
kissed her.

Four days after these curious incidents, a
funeral started from Canterville Chase at
별난, 특이한, 기이한   사건
장례식
about eleven o'clock at night.

The hearse was drawn by eight black horses,
영구차   끌다   8   검은 말
each of which carried on its head a great tuft of
각각, 각자   머리   다발
nodding ostrich-plumes, and the leaden coffin
까닥거리는   타조 깃털   납으로 만든 관
was covered by a rich purple pall, on which was
덮다   진한[짙은] 보라[자주] 관을 덮는 천
embroidered in gold the Canterville coat-of-
수를 놓다   문장(紋章)
arms.

By the side of the hearse and the coaches
영구차   마차
walked the servants with lighted torches, and
하인   횃불
the whole procession was wonderfully impres-
행진, 행렬   인상적인, 인상[감명] 깊은
sive.

Lord Canterville was the chief mourner, having come up specially from Wales to attend the
funeral, and sat in the first carriage along with
little Virginia.

Then came the United States Minister and
his wife, then Washington and the three boys,
and in the last carriage was Mrs. Umney. It was
generally felt that, as she had been frightened
by the ghost for more than fifty years of her life,
she had a right to see the last of him.

A deep grave had been dug in the corner of
the churchyard, just under the old yew-tree,
and the service was read in the most impressive
manner by the Rev. Augustus Dampier.

When the ceremony was over, the servants,
according to an old custom observed in the Canterville family, extinguished their torches, and,
as the coffin was being lowered into the grave,
Virginia stepped forward, and laid on it a large
cross made of white and pink almond-blossoms.
As she did so, the moon came out from behind a

cloud, and flooded with its silent silver the little churchyard, and from a distant copse a nightingale began to sing. She thought of the ghost's description of the Garden of Death, her eyes became dim with tears, and she hardly spoke a word during the drive home.

The next morning, before Lord Canterville went up to town, Mr. Otis had an interview with him on the subject of the jewels the ghost had given to Virginia. They were perfectly magnificent, especially a certain ruby necklace with old Venetian setting, which was really a superb specimen of sixteenth-century work, and their value was so great that Mr. Otis felt considerable scruples about allowing his daughter to accept them.

"My lord," he said, "I know that in this country mortmain is held to apply to trinkets as well as to land, and it is quite clear to me that these jewels are, or should be, heirlooms in your family. I must beg you, accordingly, to take them to

London with you, and to regard them simply as
a portion of your property which has been re-
stored to you under certain strange conditions.
As for my daughter, she is merely a child, and
has as yet, I am glad to say, but little interest in
such appurtenances of idle luxury.

"I am also informed by Mrs. Otis, who, I may
say, is no mean authority upon Art,—having had
the privilege of spending several winters in Boston when she was a girl,—that these gems are
of great monetary worth, and if offered for sale
would fetch a tall price. Under these circums
tances, Lord Canterville, I feel sure that you will
recognize how impossible it would be for me to
allow them to remain in the possession of any
member of my family; and, indeed, all such vain
gauds and toys, however suitable or necessary to
the dignity of the British aristocracy, would be
completely out of place among those who have
been brought up on the severe, and I believe im-
mortal, principles of Republican simplicity.

211

"Perhaps I should mention that Virginia is very anxious that you should allow her to retain the box, as a memento of your unfortunate but misguided ancestor. As it is extremely old, and consequently a good deal out of repair, you may perhaps think fit to comply with her request. For my own part, I confess I am a good deal sur-prised to find a child of mine expressing sympa-thy with medievalism in any form, and can only account for it by the fact that Virginia was born in one of your London suburbs shortly after Mrs. Otis had returned from a trip to Athens."

Lord Canterville listened very gravely to the worthy Minister's speech, pulling his grey moustache now and then to hide an involuntary smile, and when Mr. Otis had ended, he shook him cordially by the hand, and said:

"My dear sir, your charming little daughter rendered my unlucky ancestor, Sir Simon, a very important service, and I and my family are much indebted to her for her marvellous cour

age and pluck. The jewels are clearly hers, and, egad, I believe that if I were heartless enough to take them from her, the wicked old fellow would be out of his grave in a fortnight, leading me the devil of a life.

"As for their being heirlooms, nothing is an heirloom that is not so mentioned in a will or legal document, and the existence of these jewels has been quite unknown. I assure you I have no more claim on them than your butler, and when Miss Virginia grows up, I dare say she will be pleased to have pretty things to wear.

"Besides, you forget, Mr. Otis, that you took the furniture and the ghost at a valuation, and anything that belonged to the ghost passed at once into your possession, as, whatever activity Sir Simon may have shown in the corridor at night, in point of law he was really dead, and you acquired his property by purchase."

Mr. Otis was a good deal distressed at Lord Canterville's refusal, and begged him to reconsider his decision, but the good-natured peer was quite firm, and finally induced the Minister to allow his daughter to retain the present the ghost had given her, and when, in the spring of 1890, the young Duchess of Cheshire was presented at the Queen's first drawing-room on the occasion of her marriage, her jewels were the universal theme of admiration.

For Virginia received the coronet, which is the reward of all good little American girls, and was married to her boy-lover as soon as he came of age. They were both so charming, and they loved each other so much, that every one was delighted at the match, except the old Marchioness of Dumbleton, who had tried to catch the Duke for one of her seven unmarried daughters, and had given no less than three expensive dinner-parties for that purpose, and, strange to say, Mr. Otis himself. Mr. Otis was extremely fond of the young Duke personally, but, theoretically, he objected to titles, and, to

use his own words, "was not without apprehen-
sion lest, amid the enervating influences of a
pleasure-loving aristocracy, the true principles
of Republican simplicity should be forgotten."

His objections, however, were completely
overruled, and I believe that when he walked up
the aisle of St. George's, Hanover Square, with
his daughter leaning on his arm, there was not a
prouder man in the whole length and breadth of
England.

The Duke and Duchess, after the honeymoon
was over, went down to Canterville Chase, and
on the day after their arrival they walked over
in the afternoon to the lonely churchyard by the
pine-woods.

There had been a great deal of difficulty at
first about the inscription on Sir Simon's tomb-
stone, but finally it had been decided to engrave
on it simply the initials of the old gentleman's
name, and the verse from the library window.

The Duchess had brought with her some
공작부인　　　　가져오다

lovely roses, which she strewed upon the grave,
장미　　　　　흩다, 흩뿌리다 (= scatter)

and after they had stood by it for some time they

strolled into the ruined chancel of the old abbey.
거닐다, 산책하다　　폐허가 된　성단소, 제단　　　　수도원, 수녀원

There the Duchess sat down on a fallen pil-
쓰러진　(둥근) 기둥

lar, while her husband lay at her feet smoking
눕다　　　　담배를 피우다

a cigarette and looking up at her beautiful eyes.

Suddenly he threw his cigarette away, took hold
던지다

of her hand, and said to her, "Virginia, a wife

should have no secrets from her husband."
비밀

"Dear Cecil! I have no secrets from you."

"Yes, you have," he answered, smiling, "you
대답하다

have never told me what happened to you when
일어나다, 발생하다

you were locked up with the ghost."
~에 감금되다

"I have never told any one, Cecil," said Vir-

ginia, gravely.
진지하게, 엄숙하게

"I know that, but you might tell me."

"Please don't ask me, Cecil, I cannot tell you.

Poor Sir Simon! I owe him a great deal. Yes,
가련한, 불쌍한　　　신세를 지고 있다, 빚지다

don't laugh, Cecil, I really do. He made me see

what Life is, and what Death signifies, and why
의미하다, 뜻하다, 나타내다

217

Love is stronger than both."

~보다 더 강한

The Duke rose and kissed his wife lovingly.

일어서다

"You can have your secret as long as I have

비밀

your heart," he murmured.

중얼거리다

"You have always had that, Cecil."

"And you will tell our children some day,

말하다, 전하다   언젠가

won't you?"

Virginia blushed.

얼굴을 붉히다, 얼굴이 빨개지다 (= go red)

📚 나만의 리뷰 and 명문장

🕮 나만의 리뷰 and 명문장

📚 나만의 리뷰 and 명문장

🐟 나만의 리뷰 and 명문장